The Coastal Companion

The Coastal Companion

A GUIDE TO THE INSIDE PASSAGE INCLUDING PUGET SOUND, BC AND ALASKA

BY JOE UPTON

Harbour Publishing

Published by
Harbour Publishing Co. Ltd., P.O. Box 219, Madeira Park, BC V0N 2H0
www.harbourpublishing.com

The maps in this book are not to be used for navigation.

Editing by Ed Reading, illustrations by Russ Burtner and Christine Cox, maps by Joe Upton, design by Martha Brouwer
Photographs and credits as noted with the following abbreviations:
    AMNH - American Museum of Natural History, New York; BCARS - British Columbia Archives and Records Service; BCRM - Royal British Columbia Museum; MOHAI - Museum of History and Industry, Seattle; SFM - San Francisco Maritime Museum; THS - Tongass Historical Society, Ketchikan, Alaska; UW - University of Washington Special Collections.
    Diary photo credits: pages 204, 205; British Columbia Archives and Records Service, page 207; University of Washington Special Collections, Thwaites 0024-F25, others by author.

Printed and bound in Canada.

Harbour Publishing acknowledges financial support from the Government of Canada through the Book Publishing Industry Development Program and the Canada Council for the Arts, and from the Province of British Columbia through the British Columbia Arts Council and the Book Publisher's Tax Credit through the Ministry of Provincial Revenue.

THE CANADA COUNCIL | LE CONSEIL DES ARTS
FOR THE ARTS | DU CANADA
SINCE 1957 | DEPUIS 1957

BRITISH
COLUMBIA
ARTS COUNCIL
Supported by the Province of British Columbia

National Library of Canada Cataloguing in Publication

Upton, Joe, 1946–
    The coastal companion: a guide to the Inside Passage, including Puget Sound, B.C. and Alaska / Joe Upton.

First published as: The coastal companion: a guide for the Alaska-bound traveler. Bainbridge Island, Wash.: Coastal Pub., 1995.
Includes bibliographical references and index.
ISBN 1-55017-324-3

    1. Inside Passage—Guidebooks. I. Title.
FC3845.I5U67 2004   917.1'11   C2004-901249-5

For
Mary Lou, Matthew,
and Katherine Anne,
mariners all.

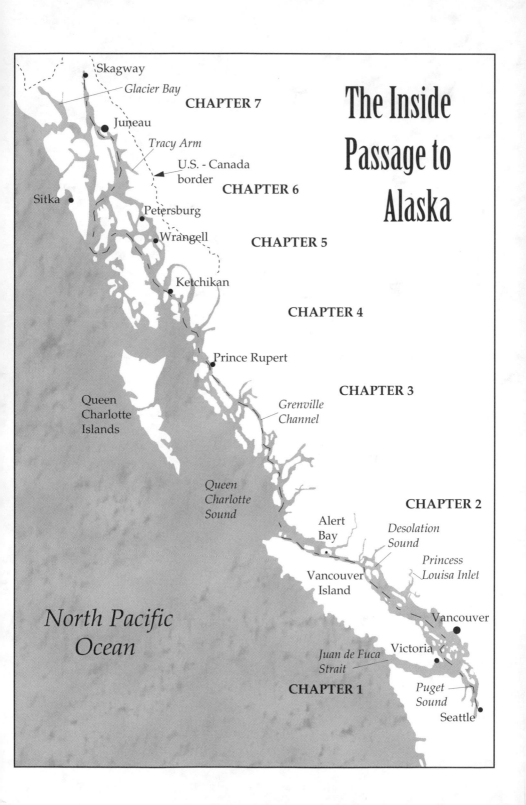

Skagway

Glacier Bay

CHAPTER 7

Juneau

Tracy Arm

U.S. - Canada
border

CHAPTER 6

Sitka

Petersburg

Wrangell

CHAPTER 5

Ketchikan

CHAPTER 4

The Inside
Passage to
Alaska

Prince Rupert

CHAPTER 3

Queen
Charlotte
Islands

*Grenville
Channel*

*Queen
Charlotte
Sound*

CHAPTER 2

Alert
Bay

*Desolation
Sound*

*Princess
Louisa Inlet*

North Pacific
Ocean

Vancouver
Island

Vancouver

Victoria

*Juan de Fuca
Strait*

*Puget
Sound*

CHAPTER 1

Seattle

Contents

Joe Upton Photos

Frederick Sound, Alaska, 1975

To the Traveler

On a June morning in 1965, 20 hours after leaving Seattle, I felt a hand on my shoulder in the darkened fo'c's'le of the *Sidney*, the Alaska-bound boat I'd just gotten my first job on.

"C'mon up, kid," the 70-year-old mate rasped, nodding up at the pilothouse stairs, "you gotta' see this."

He was right. We lay almost motionless in a little bight in a steep and forested shore. Ahead of us in the thin dawn light I could make out a wild torrent of water, like rapids in a river, pouring out of a gap in the trees. I lowered a window and looked out. A deep roaring sound filled the air, echoing off the walls of the canyon that surrounded us.

"W-w-we're going th-th-there..?" I stammered, awed at the sight, inexperienced and totally new to the Inside Passage.

"It used to be really bad," came the soft-voiced answer, "That's Seymour Narrows. There was a rock right in the middle. They blew it the hell out of there. Watch now, here comes a few fellows...."

Just then two good-sized boats tumbled through the gap, heeling one way and then the other as they struggled in the current, skirting the big whirlpools just off our stern.

The *Sidney* is gone now, burned up and sunk somewhere in the Bering Sea. And my old shipmate Mickey, who took pity on a green kid and taught me about Seymour and a hundred other places on wheel watches through that endless island wilderness, has passed on too.

But that long season in the north and that kindly older gentleman instilled in me a lifelong interest in northern places and history, especially the inland waterways that form the Inside Passage and Southeast Alaska.

Now, almost three decades, 11 boats, and three books from where I started, I fly to the remote tundra coast of western Alaska each spring. Meet my crew, rig our nets, launch our boat, and fish the shallow rivers for salmon, with the volcanos of the Alaska Peninsula steaming, brillant white on the horizon.

On the plane I get a window seat, and if it's clear I look down as the coast passes beneath.

Mickey and me, aboard the Sidney, 1965.

Tucked beneath the the wall of the Fairweather Range, I make out the exquisite basin of Lituya Bay, where the French explorer Lapérouse lost two of his small boats and 21 brave men in the tide rips in 1786. We pass over iceberg-dotted Glacier Bay, and I imagine it as John Muir had discovered it in 1879 : a stunning, wild and magic place. I look north and east, to the very head of Lynn Canal, the village of Skagway and the trailhead where thousands of gold-hungry men in '97 and '98 had first glimpsed the hardships that lay ahead.

The plane continues south, over the canyon that was Chatham Strait, over bays and coves where I'd fished, hunted, and explored. At the north end of Prince of Wales Island, I pick out Port Protection, the cove where Captain Vancouver and his ships found desperately needed shelter in the last minutes before a powerful storm in 1793, and where I built a cabin and lived in the roadless wilderness 180 years later.

We slant farther to the east, and I make out the big mill at Ketchikan and then the ethereal shapes of the mountains and the water at Misty Fjords and Portland Canal, where Vancouver had such a hard time tracing the continental boundary.

Then, but for the occasional flash from a lighthouse, all is darkness until finally the plane slows, and we begin our descent. The lights of Vancouver and Victoria, Bellingham and Seattle fill the night beneath us and the spell of the North is broken.

As I worked along this coast, it was my habit to seek out the little-visited, out-of-the-way places. Go ashore when the wind blew, explore, beachcomb, visit. And so over the years I acquired a keen sense of the coast, in most of its many moods.

So, come, take this journey. Share a sense of what went before, of the mystery, the power of this place that remains much as it was when the first explorers passed through.

MOHAI

Launch Foxy *in Puget Sound, Washington, about 1920. By picking their route and weather carefully, skippers of such small craft could travel to Alaska via the Inside Passage.*

The Inside Passage

To a mariner, "inside" means "protected," and when the Pleistocene glaciers scoured out the fjords and canyons of the northwest coast a million years ago, they created "protected" waters and a boater's paradise.

Behind the eight large islands between Cape Flattery, Washington, and Cape Spencer, Alaska, is a roughly northwest-southeast route that has become known as the Inside Passage. Stretching for a thousand miles from Seattle, Washington, to Skagway, Alaska, it allows small and large craft alike to travel in protection and comfort.

The Inside Passage was explored, charted, and named in the 1790s by a British Navy captain, George Vancouver, who sought a sea route from west to east.

In some places, vessels have a choice of routes. For the purposes of this book, the "Inside Passage" means the traditional route laid out for small and medium-size craft in the *Hansen Handbook* (see page 26), now out of print but once an essential navigational guide for mariners before the days of modern electronics.

The Tides

A channel marker in Wrangell Narrows at Petersburg. Here savvy mariners tie up their boats before they put their engines into neutral. At times the current past the docks can run at four knots (about four and a half miles an hour) which is faster than you can walk.

In few waterways of the world does the tide so influence mariners as it does along the northwest coast. From the tipsy sailor who exits a tavern, only to face the 45-degree ramp down to his boat, to the skipper of a 6,000-horsepower tug who steams to the side of Johnstone Strait when the current is against him, the mariner here must always consider the tide.

In the Kvichak River of western Alaska, propellers of boats at anchor are turned by the tide. In Sergius Narrows, near Sitka, Coast Guard buoys disappear underwater, pulled down by the current when the tide is running.

In some constricted passages, the tide rushes with a force like rapids in a river. In Seymour Narrows and Yuculta Rapids, British Columbia, safe passage is possible only briefly each day: at slack water, the top or the bottom of the tide.

Tides are caused by moon's gravity (and to a lesser extent the sun's) pulling earth's oceans into bulges on either side that attempt to follow the moon. Because the moon takes one day plus 50 minutes to orbit the earth, each tide is 50 minutes later than the day before.

Tides on this coast have a great range of rise and fall, from 10 feet in Seattle to 18 feet in Ketchikan, Alaska. At certain times of the year, the alignment of moon, sun, and planets create tides higher and lower.

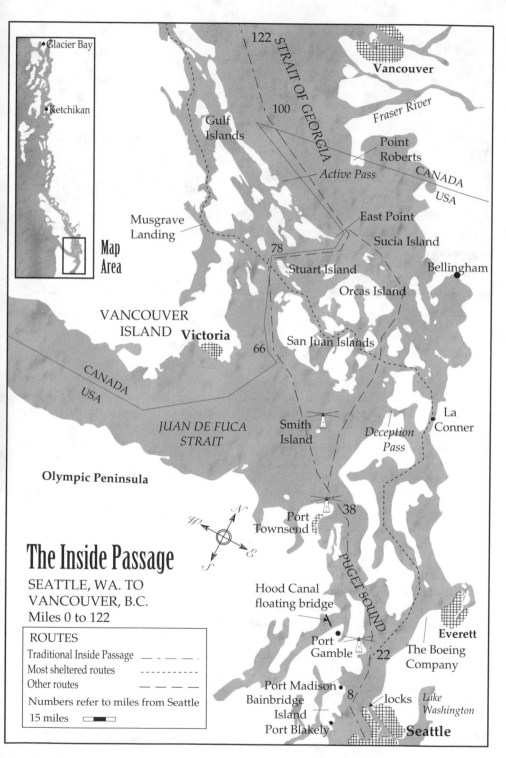

Glacier Bay

Ketchikan

Map Area

122 STRAIT OF GEORGIA

Vancouver

100

Fraser River

Gulf Islands

Point Roberts

Active Pass

CANADA
USA

Musgrave Landing

East Point

Sucia Island

78

Stuart Island

Bellingham

Orcas Island

VANCOUVER ISLAND **Victoria**

66

San Juan Islands

CANADA
USA

JUAN DE FUCA STRAIT

Smith Island

Deception Pass

La Conner

Olympic Peninsula

N
W E
S

38

Port Townsend

PUGET SOUND

The Inside Passage

SEATTLE, WA. TO VANCOUVER, B.C.
Miles 0 to 122

Hood Canal floating bridge

Everett

The Boeing Company

Port Gamble

22

ROUTES

Traditional Inside Passage — · — · —
Most sheltered routes - - - - - -
Other routes — — — —
Numbers refer to miles from Seattle
15 miles ▭

Port Madison
Bainbridge Island
Port Blakely

8

locks

Lake Washington

Seattle

CHAPTER 1

Seattle to Vancouver
MILE 0 TO MILE 113

Seattle, May 11, 1973: The last jobs have been done, the last things bought, the last goodbyes said. Our little boat lies still in the water tonight, freshly painted, engine and electronics tuned, every cubby and corner jammed full of supplies, ready for a long season. Tonight, the roar of the traffic. Tomorrow, the stillness of the North. Away in the morning, away for Alaska!

The Inside Passage begins in Seattle at Colman Dock. It's Pier 52, or **mile 0** of the route described in Captain Farwell's *Hansen Handbook* (see page 26). From here, thousands of gold-hungry men embarked on a journey to the Alaska and Klondike gold fields that changed so many lives in 1897 and 1898.

The harbor landmark was the big, lighted clock tower on Colman Dock. But in 1912 the steamship *Alameda* sliced through the dock, knocked the clock tower into the water, and sank a stern-wheeler tied up on the other side.

On today's waterfront, look for the ferries. Puget Sound has one of the largest ferry systems in the world, with 24 of the green and white double-ended vessels serving nine routes. Busiest is the Bainbridge Island ferry to Seattle, where 2,000 commuters and 210 cars squeeze aboard for the 35-minute rush-hour sailings across Elliott Bay. They sail from Colman Dock, too, but practical as these Northwesterners are the clock tower has never been replaced.

Tens of thousands of commuters cross Puget Sound by ferry each day.

The beach around the first point to the south at **mile 2** is Alki. It was here that the Denny party, Seattle's first settlers, slogged ashore in a rainstorm in November 1851. The

Look for the green and white tugboats with this profile—they have no propellers. (See page 70)

Puget Sound tribes subsisted primarily on seafood

women of the party, who'd spent the previous six months struggling with the rigors of the Oregon Trail, broke into tears when they saw the promised land: a roofless cabin at the edge of a gloomy forest, a rough-looking Chief Sealth and members of his Suquamish tribe waiting to greet them.

If they had looked around them they might have noticed an evergreen tree with peculiar flat needles, not seen in the East: the Douglas fir, or Oregon Pine ("Doug fir" in the lumber business). It was the foundation of the Northwest's principal industry for the next century.

Less than a month later, the sailing ship *Leonesa* dropped anchor, and her skipper offered the party $1,000 cash for a load of 50-foot fir piles. The settlers sharpened their axes and an industry was born.

Puget Sound is like a northwest Chesapeake Bay: a many-armed waterway, very urban in places, rural in others, but deeper and surrounded by high mountains. The new Puget Sound is along the Seattle-Tacoma-Everett corridor: fast-growing, fast-paced, busy, noisy, even polluted in places.

The old Puget Sound of cedar bungalows and wooden boats, forests sloping to the water's edge, driftwood fires, eagles, and native settlements lingers mostly in the western and southern sound. The smell of the sea and the woods, a long log raft headed to a mill, a graceful salmon boat setting a net on a gray and drizzly summer morning, and Mount Rainier breaking suddenly through the overcast, dazzlingly bright—these are the elements that make the Puget Sound country unusual.

At **mile** 3 is the place, according to local lore, where a destroyer captain tried to drop anchor and failed. Recently arrived from the East Coast, where depths are charted in feet,

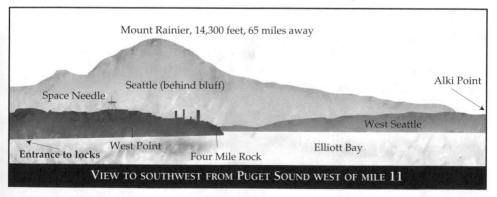

VIEW TO SOUTHWEST FROM PUGET SOUND WEST OF MILE 11

SFM

he thought he was in a hundred feet of water. In the deep waters of the Northwest, chart depths are marked in fathoms, each fathom equaling six feet, and he was in a hundred fathoms of water.

The 10,000-pound anchor thundered into the bay, followed by its chain. The crew waited for the anchor to hit bottom before applying the winch brakes. Realizing that something was very wrong, the sailors ran from the dangerously overspeeding winch as the last of the chain, the end painted red as a warning, roared out of the chain locker, ripping the welded eye off the deck and taking part of the destroyer's bow with it, and disappeared into the water.

Look to the south as you leave Seattle. That brilliant white cone (seen on clear days) is Mount Rainier, the 14,300-foot volcano looming over Puget Sound. The remarkably symmetrical Rainier is part of a volcanic chain stretch-

This is a harbor? At Big River, California, in 1903, the steam schooner Phoenix loads lumber by overhead cable. The lack of good harbors along the ocean coasts of California, Oregon, and Washington made Puget Sound lumber very attractive.

The Brothers, 6,920 feet , 36 miles

Kitsap Peninsula

Olympic Peninsula

Bainbridge Island

Eagle Harbor

Puget Sound

VIEW TO WEST FROM QUENN ANNE HILL, EAST OF MILE 4

The sawmills at Port Blakely and other harbors began an industry that was to dominate the Northwest for almost a century.

ing south to California that includes Mount Baker, Mount St. Helens, Mount Adams, and Mount Hood.

These volcanoes were considered extinct until 8:18 on a Sunday morning in May 1980. After two months of throat-clearing, Mount St. Helens blew 1,300 feet of mountain and a cubic mile of ash into the atmosphere. The explosion and ensuing landslides and floods killed 57 people and knocked flat several million trees.

Look for fishing boats exiting the Hiram Chittenden Locks at the marina on the eastern shore, **mile 7**. The locks lead from Lake Washington and Lake Union, winter shelter for much of the Alaskan fishing fleet.

Across from Seattle, what looks like solid shoreline is Bainbridge Island. On Bainbridge at Port Blakely was built the first of the big sawmills that made Puget Sound the lumber capital of the world for a century. The combination of huge, straight-grained trees growing close to the tidewater in sheltered harbors was perfect. The timber went to California, where the population was exploding with the Gold Rush of 1849.

On the western shore opposite **mile 8**, Port Madison winds back into the interior of Bainbridge Island; only six

The First 707

Gold Cup Day, on August 7, 1955, was the highlight of the annual Seafair. Some 250,000 spectators, including members of the International Air Transport Association and the Society of Aeronautical Engineers, who were in town for a conference, stood on boats and on the shore to watch the unlimited hydroplanes race on Lake Washington.

The sound of a jet approaching low and fast from the west made the crowd look up. What they saw remained etched in memory.

The new Boeing 707 airliner, first ever built, which was being flight-tested that day, approached at 500 miles per hour in a shallow dive, right over the race course. Then, as the crowd gasped, the huge airplane pulled up smoothly into a steep climb, rolled slowly on its back and did a perfect barrel roll. Then it turned back over the crowd and did one again.

The pilot, Tex Johnston, said later that as Boeing's competitors were telling airlines the big jet was unstable, he figured a demonstration of the aircraft's capability was in order. Watching from the ground, the Boeing president, Bill Allen, probably had to take a heart pill when he saw the precious airplane on which the company had bet its future perform the unplanned maneuver.

Jan Fardell

miles from the Hiram Chittenden Locks, it's a favorite overnight spot for Seattle yachtsmen.

DID YOU KNOW? Washington State has 3,026 miles of tidal shoreline, the tenth longest in the United States. Alaska is first with 31,383 miles; Florida is second with 8,426.

Over the bluff six miles east of **mile 18** is the engine that drove Puget Sound's economy during the 1960s and '70s, less so today: The Boeing Company, jet builder to the world.

Look for Point No Point lighthouse to the west at **mile 22**; its radar antenna is part of the Puget Sound Vessel Traffic System, the maritime equivalent to an air traffic control system. So many fast freighters use the sound that special traffic lanes have been set up to separate the northbound and southbound traffic. Two container ships approaching head to head, for example, would have a closing speed of more than 40 miles an hour.

Foulweather Bluff, to the west at **mile 25**, hides the entrance to 60-mile-long, elbow-shaped Hood Canal, a popu-

A Northwest landmark gone in minutes: Spirit Lake and Mount St. Helens are seen in better days. The graceful lodges and peaceful lake were destroyed, along with the upper third of the mountain, in an explosive eruption on May 18, 1980.

The Arrival of Vancouver

"April 29, 1792. At four o'clock [a.m.] a sail was discovered to the westward standing in shore. This was a very great novelty, not having seen any vessel but our consort, during the last eight months. She soon hoisted American colors and fired a gun to leeward." —Captain George Vancouver, *A Voyage of Discovery to the North Pacific Ocean and Round the World.*

This was a singular day for the British captain and his two ships and crews. They had sailed from England 15 months earlier to seek the Northwest Passage from the Pacific Ocean to the Atlantic. Vancouver had his doubts. Captain Cook hadn't found it and Vancouver was with him. For 6,000 miles, almost to the southern tip of Chile, the Pacific coast was a wall, with no interior straits and few good harbors.

The American vessel [Captain Robert Gray, a Boston fur trader, in the *Columbia*] assured them the strait existed; it was a few miles to the north. Around noon on the 29th the rain and the mists parted and Vancouver saw it: the Strait! 10 miles wide, 500 feet deep, it led east between high, snowy mountains. He thought it was the Northwest Passage.

At that time, Philadelphia and Boston had cobblestone streets and daily newspapers, yet the known world ended west of the Missouri River; beyond that was marked "unknown" on the maps. Another 13 years would pass before Lewis and Clark would uncover the vastness and the beauty of the American west.

A week after entering the strait that turned out to be *not* the Northwest Passage, the Vancouver party—continually charting and exploring, following the shore to make sure they missed no channel that might lead to the Atlantic—turned south and entered a waterway Vancouver named for one of his lieutenants, Peter Puget. Vancouver was stunned by what he saw.

"I could not possibly believe that any uncultivated country had ever been discovered exhibiting so rich a picture.... To describe the beauties of this region, will, on some future occasion, be a very grateful task to the pen of a skillful panegyrist. The serenity of the climate, the innumerable pleasing landscapes, and the abundant fertility that unassisted nature puts forth, require only to be enriched by the industry of man with villages, mansions, cottages, and other buildings, to render it the most lovely country that can be imagined; whilst the labor of the inhabitants would be amply rewarded, in the bounties which nature seems ready to bestow on cultivation." —George Vancouver, *A Voyage of Discovery.*

The entrance to the Northwest Passage could be small, he thought. In order not to miss it, Vancouver followed the continental boundary, exploring, charting, but always following the shore. When he arrived in Puget Sound and saw the myriad channels and passages leading off in all directions, it was obvious to him that the task was too difficult for the cumbersome ships *Discovery* and *Chatham*. The solution lay in small boats, his 20-foot cutters, rigged to row and sail. The big boats would anchor and the small boats would set out, sometimes with Vancouver and sometimes without, charting the vast land they had discovered.

SFM

Look at the size of that timber: A 22-by-22-inch by 79-foot piece of fir being loaded for England at Port Blakely, probably for use in a ship's keel. Such a timber would be unobtainable today, unless perhaps salvaged from an old building.

lar summering spot. Look sharp and you might see a 560-foot Trident submarine from the sub base at Bangor.

The land to the west, from **mile 29** to mile 35, is Marrowstone Island, where Captain Vancouver found another of the arrangements of tall poles, usually across low beaches between higher land, that puzzled him. Later he determined that the natives used the poles to hang nets to capture passing birds.

The town to the west at **mile 38** is Port Townsend. According to the real estate sharps in the 1880s, Port Townsend was certain to be the western terminus of the Northern Pacific Railway, which was then advancing across the plains. A lot of land was sold to speculators before the bubble burst with the announcement that Tacoma was selected instead. Look for gracious Victorian houses with gingerbread trim on the bluff at Port Townsend.

Look for tide rips, too, which occur when the wind and the tidal current oppose one another, or when these currents accelerate in constricted passages.

Watch out for tide rips at Point Wilson.

Puget Sound proper ends at **mile 40**, Point Wilson. Wherever tidal currents turn a corner, as they do here, they are apt to swirl and eddy, causing the so-called tide rips. When they are opposed by a wind, these currents can produce conditions that are difficult for small craft. Native travelers in canoes held the Point Wilson tide rip with particular regard. It is reported that the paddlers sat very still and paddled carefully to avoid disturbing the god of tide rips and safe passages.

TIPS FOR MARINERS: The tidal currents split south of the San Juan Islands, flooding in from the ocean and turning both north into Canadian waters and south into Puget Sound. Headed up into Canada? Take advantage of this: ride the ebbing current north out of Puget Sound, catch the change near Smith Island, **mile 50**, and then ride the north-flowing flood up into the Strait of Georgia.

The Maggie Murphy

For many young people, growing up on Puget Sound and hearing the stories of Alaska and the North from those who had been there, the itch to follow was strong. In the 1930s two teenagers, John Joseph Ryan and Ed Braddock, salvaged a derelict 26-footer from the mud flats at Tacoma, rebuilt it as best they could (thanks to the unknowing help of a nearby lumber mill), and set out up the Inside Passage. They had barely reached Seattle when one of the flaws of their vessel revealed itself.

"First of all, the pilothouse proved to be utterly uninhabitable. It had about two inches less headroom than was needed to permit either of us to stand erect while steering; the engine was right underfoot, belching fumes and heat that rose up to smother the helmsman; furthermore, there was no danger that either fumes or heat would escape because the windows had been nailed and puttied in place, sealing the pilothouse as tight as a mummy's crypt." —John Joseph Ryan, *The Maggie Murphy*

Author's collection

Would you want to go to Alaska in this rig? These men did.

MOHAI

The wing room, the Boeing Airplane Company, Seattle, 1920s. Workers are fabricating wing sections out of Sitka spruce, to be covered by fabric. The construction of a series of dams along the Columbia River in the 1930s and 1940s allowed the cheap production of aluminum which was to radically change the manufacture of aircraft.

Look for Juan de Fuca Strait, 10 miles wide and 50 miles long, visible to the west from **mile 40** to about **mile 55**. Looks big, but Captain Cook and other early explorers missed it.

Does it really rain that much here? Ironically, Seattle, with 38 inches of rain annually, gets less than New York's 43 inches or

Mount Baker, 10,778 feet, distance 44 miles

Orcas Island

Obstruction Island

Obstruction Pass

VIEW TO NE NEAR OBSTRUCTION PASS, SAN JUAN ISLANDS, 4 MI WEST OF MILE 56E

Look for vessels entering and exiting narrow island passes.

soggy Kansas City's 50 inches. It's just that it's spread out over so much of the year that it seems it rains a lot.

Crossing the strait at **mile 39**: The tide can make this passage difficult for small craft. A cubic mile of water has to pass on a big tide, creating currents that can get ugly if the wind's blowing. In the summer, as the land masses inland heat up, the air rises, drawing cooler ocean air through the strait. Westerly winds rise in early afternoon and blow hard until after dark.

Look for Deception Pass, much used by small craft, under the bridge east of **mile 58E**. Thatcher Pass, west of **mile 67E**, is used by the San Juan Islands-to-Anacortes ferries. The refineries southeast of **mile 68E** and east of **mile 88E** are supplied by tankers carrying crude oil from Alaska. In these waters tankers are accompanied by powerful tugs in case of loss of power.

SPECIAL PLACES: Like an inland canal, the Swinomish Channel cuts through the Skagit River delta farm country near La Conner (20 miles east of **mile 66**), a sort of arts, fishing, tourist, farming community. In April, when thousands of

Native Culture and the Coming of the Whites

Before Cook and Vancouver, before the tide of whites that flooded into the region in the 1800s, Puget Sound natives had lived thousands of years in a culture that, compared to other native Americans, could only be described as idyllic. The sea and the forest provided.

There was cedar for houses, and halibut, salmon, herring, whales, eulachon (a herring-like fish harvested for its oil), clams and berries for food. They had no agriculture; they didn't need it. They were hunter-gatherers but they could gather food without the nomadic life of their Plains brothers. (They might, however, move each spring to summer villages near the mouths of salmon streams.)

The coming of the white man brought something worse than the loss of their lands; it brought a plague like that which swept Europe in the Middle Ages. Who first brought smallpox and tuberculosis to the Northwest Indians? Was it a Spaniard, or a "Boston man" from Gray's ship? Captain Cook's sailmaker or Vancouver's gunner?

It mattered little; when the first sail appeared over the horizon in the 1770s, the curtain was about to be drawn on a powerful culture that had endured for centuries.

Joe Upton

The signal event that put Alaska and Seattle on the map was the 1897 discovery of gold along the tributaries of Canada's Yukon River. U.S. prospector George Carmack actually made the discovery in August, 1896, but the news didn't reach the United States until 1897. Tens of thousands of men came to Seattle to buy their outfits and head north aboard a fleet of aging steamers.

acres of tulips and daffodils blossom, the scents and vibrant colors of this waterway are almost overwhelming.

From **mile 60** to mile 100, the Inside Passage parallels the Canadian border west of the San Juan Islands, and passes into Canadian waters in the Strait of Georgia.

The border used to be farther north, along the 49th parallel about 15 miles south of Vancouver. Although it was an easy line to draw inland, the border had wrinkles when it hit the coast. The whole southern tip of Vancouver Island, for instance, including Victoria, its main English settlement, would have been in the United States, so in 1846 negotiators settled for a line down the middle of the channel.

The San Juan Islands archipelago of 172 islands, small

The San Juan Islands are extremely popular with yachtsmen.

Trouble with Bridges

The water depth in Puget Sound poses a particular problem to bridge builders. Had the sound been as shallow as Chesapeake Bay, for instance, no doubt there would be a cross-sound bridge. But with depths to 800 feet and distances of three miles from shore to shore, a pile-supported or suspension bridge was impossible.

The solution, at least for the narrower crossings, was floating bridges, built on massive concrete floats and moored to huge anchors. Impressive-looking, they were, however, vulnerable.

The first bridge to sink was the Hood Canal Floating Bridge, which did so on February 13, 1979. Since it was exposed to the long sweep of waves that a storm would drive up the canal, the bridge was designed to be opened in a storm to relieve pressure on the windward side. The opening was made by retracting part of the floating structure back into itself. The opening also allowed passage of the 560-foot Trident submarines to their West Coast base at Bangor, 10 miles south. The canal was deep enough for the subs to travel submerged, but threading through the bridge's mooring cables submerged would have been too dangerous.

On that stormy February night, when the bridge tender tried to open the bridge to ease the strain, the mechanism failed to work, and as he watched in astonishment part of the floating portions of the bridge sank.

Next to go was one of the Lake Washington bridges. It lay on a key commuter link between Seattle and its rapidly growing east-side suburbs, which induced enough traffic flowing across the lake during rush hour to require a pair of four-lane bridges, the busiest route being Interstate 90.

Imagine the consternation of east-siders with water-view property as they looked out from their 1991 Thanksgiving dinners while a violent 60-mile-per-hour gale swept the city. One of the two bridges sank, section after section, as they watched.

Of course, to Puget Sound folk, collapsing bridges were not new. Although it was a suspension bridge rather than a floating bridge, the Tacoma Narrows Bridge broke up and fell into the sound on November 7, 1940, just four months after it opened. This is probably the most dramatic engineering failure in modern United States history.

The graceful, three-quarter-mile-long Golden Gate look-alike crossed Puget Sound west of Tacoma, 35 miles south of Seattle. Its particularly graceful aspect was due to its unusually shallow deck, which had fewer bracing members below the roadway than other bridges its size. The design was an unfortunate choice. The Narrows are notoriously windy, and the bridge soon became known as Galloping Gertie, for the way she twisted and bucked in storms.

The roadway would oscillate in waves so high that one could lose sight of the car ahead. They tried parking heavily loaded trucks on the bridge to damp the motion while the engineers grappled with what to do.

Gertie didn't wait. On the particularly windy day it failed, the bridge was bucking so badly that one driver had to abandon his car and run for it, knocked down again and again by the bucking roadway. It's good he was a strong runner; the bridge deck collapsed and fell into the water behind him.

MOHAI

and large, bucolic and sleepy for most of the year, is transformed each summer as boaters and summer folk arrive from the Puget Sound cities to the south.

The city visible 14 miles west of mile 60 is Victoria, the British Columbia capital. It is an unusually graceful and accessible small city, its downtown within walking distance of the lakelike inner harbor. In earlier days, life there had a few rough edges:

> "I have witnessed scenes after sunset calculated to shock even the bluntest sensibilities. The fires of Indian tents pitched upon the beach casting a lurid glare upon the water; the loud and discordant whoopings of the natives, several of whom were usually infuriated with bad liquor; the crowds of the more debased miners strewed in vicious concert with squaws on the public highway, presented a spectacle diabolical in the extreme."
> —Matthew Macfie, *Vancouver Island and British Columbia: Their History, Resources, and Prospects*, London, 1865.

Galloping Gertie, aka the Tacoma Narrows Bridge, shaking herself to pieces on November 7, 1940. In 1979 the Hood Canal Floating Bridge sank, followed in 1991 by the Interstate 90 floating bridge.

Portion of the 1930s Hansen Handbook, *a compilation of courses, distances, sketches, and so forth, that allowed mariners to travel the Inside Passage without having to carry a complete and expensive set of charts.*

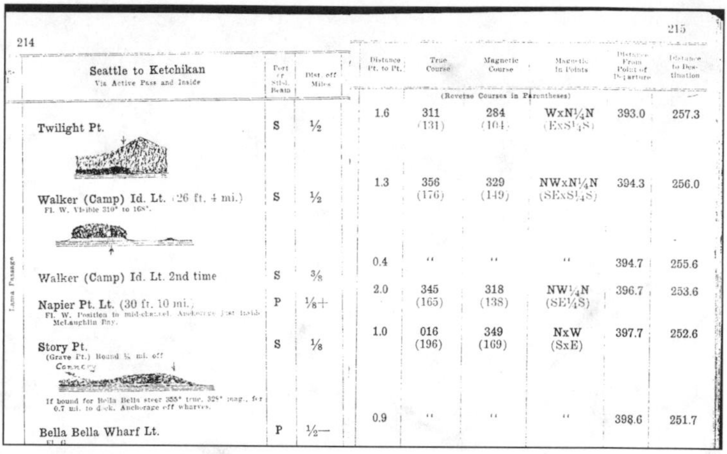

214 | 215

Seattle to Ketchikan Via Active Pass and Inside	Port or Stbd. Beam	Dist. off Miles	Distance Pt. to Pt.	True Course	Magnetic Course	Magnetic In Points	Distance From Point of Departure	Distance to Destination
			(Reverse Courses in Parentheses)					
Twilight Pt.	S	½	1.6	311 (131)	284 (104)	WxN¼N (ExS¼S)	393.0	257.3
Walker (Camp) Id. Lt. (26 ft. 4 mi.) Fl. W. Visible 310° to 168°.	S	½	1.3	356 (176)	329 (149)	NWxN¼N (SExS¼S)	394.3	256.0
Walker (Camp) Id. Lt. 2nd time	S	⅜	0.4	"	"	"	394.7	255.6
Napier Pt. Lt. (30 ft. 10 mi.) Fl. W. Position in mid-channel. Anchorage just inside McLaughlin Bay.	P	⅛+	2.0	345 (165)	318 (138)	NW¼N (SE¼S)	396.7	253.6
Story Pt. (Grave Pt.) Round ⅛ mi. off. Cannery. If bound for Bella Bella steer 355° true, 328° mag., for 0.7 mi. to dock. Anchorage off wharves.	S	⅛	1.0	016 (196)	349 (169)	NxW (SxE)	397.7	252.6
Bella Bella Wharf Lt. Fl. G.	P	½—	0.9	"	"	"	398.6	251.7

Lama Passage

At Pedder Bay, 10 miles southwest of Victoria, the only albino killer whale ever captured, Chimo, was taken in March 1970.

Watch for ferry traffic in Active Pass.

Look for the lighthouse at Turn Point, **mile 78.** The border and the Inside Passage turn sharply east here. Look for killer whales or orcas (see pages 57 and 203), in the tide rips here.

ACTIVE PASS OR BOUNDARY PASS?

North of the San Juans, ships have a choice of routes. Large ships stay in big water: Boundary Pass, two miles wide, with a three- to five-knot current, will accommodate the largest ships. Small boats jog north at Turn Point and wind through the Gulf Islands to Active Pass, **mile 90.**

You'll want to have a look at Active Pass. *Pass* is the name given to the narrow, deep channels between islands, and of all those on the northwest coast, Active Pass is the

A Mosquito Fleet

In the early years of this century, dozens of small steamboats, a "mosquito fleet," people said, provided transportation up and down the sound.

Racing the rival steamboat was great sport. The engine room crews on wood-fired boats kept a stash of extra-hot-burning resin- and pitch-filled wood slabs for those moments when an opponent hove into sight.

Before radar came along in the 1940s, the little steamboats tried to keep to their schedules by any means, fog or not. The more astute skippers felt their way along by tooting their whistles and horns and listening for the echoes off the land and for the answering cries of animals along the way.

Raytheon Marine

busiest and the most dramatic. Its steep shores, right-angle turns, fast ferry traffic, and seven-knot tidal current make for plenty of excitement.

The challenge for large ships, especially the Vancouver-to-Victoria ferries, is maintaining steerage way in the currents. The only way to do this is to travel fairly fast. But the large ships have such tremendous mass and momentum they may travel more than halfway across the constricted channel, rudder full over, before completing their turn. Mariners in small craft who approach the pass, with its S-curves and blind corners, have to be ready to give the fast-moving ferries plenty of room. Ferry skippers usually sound the horn when they enter the pass and notify the other traffic on VHF Channel 16.

If your ship takes the Boundary Pass route, look sharp to see the narrow entrance to Active Pass west of **mile 93**, about a half hour after you make the big right-angle turn to the northwest in Boundary Pass.

DID YOU KNOW? The 49th parallel, which is the United States-Canada border, makes the lower 2,000 acres of the Point Roberts peninsula part of the United States.

SPECIAL PLACES: Sucia and Matia Islands, two state park islands five miles southeast of Boundary Pass at **mile 88E** are true gems. Sucia is a mini-archipelago, one large and eight smaller

Wouldn't the old-timers have loved this a battery powered, waterproof global positioning system (GPS) chart plotter. It displays your position on an electronic chart. Before the development of electronic navigation aids such as radar and loran, finding the Juan de Fuca Strait in thick weather was hazardous.

Sucia and Matia Islands are ideal for boat camping

Many salmon vessels work near the mouth of the Fraser River.

islands, purchased by a group of yacht clubs and boating enthusiasts and given to the state park system. The beauty of Fossil Bay with the late afternoon summer sun streaming in over the anchorages and campsites, with children swimming and playing and paddling small craft among the shallows, is compelling.

Matia ("Matey") is considerably smaller and, with room only for a few boats, much quieter. The westernmost cove is small and private, with unusual smoothed rock formations; it has a few campsites on the bluff overlooking the water.

Look for milky water from the mighty Fraser River, which roars down through the mountains in dramatic canyons and gorges, but sputters into the Strait of Georgia across a wide, muddy delta. It is visible to the northeast at around **mile 100**. The Fraser is a big river, second only to the Columbia on the West Coast, but narrow at its mouth.

Look for salmon gill-netters in this area, setting their drift nets for red, or sockeye, salmon. The border between the United States and Canada takes a big dogleg here, allowing American fishermen to creep almost to the river's mouth. The Fraser was a huge producer of red salmon before 1914. Then, landslides caused by construction of the Canadian Northern Railway through Hell's Gate Canyon made fish passage up the 110-foot-wide slot in the mountains almost impossible. Only recently, after decades of hatchery-building and stream improvement, have the salmon runs come back to their pre-landslide levels.

During spring and early summer, the peculiarly milky water of the Fraser River carries across the Strait of Georgia into Active Pass.

Campsite at Fossil Bay, Sucia Island marine park.

San Juans Scrapbook

The store at Olga, Orcas Island. Lopez Island in distance.

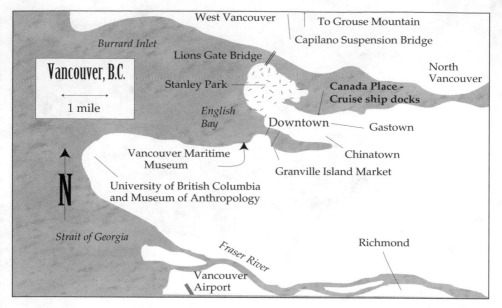

West Vancouver

To Grouse Mountain

Burrard Inlet

Capilano Suspension Bridge

Lions Gate Bridge

North Vancouver

Stanley Park

Canada Place - Cruise ship docks

English Bay

Downtown

Gastown

Vancouver Maritime Museum

Chinatown

Granville Island Market

University of British Columbia and Museum of Anthropology

Strait of Georgia

Fraser River

Richmond

Vancouver Airport

If you do nothing else, take a walk through spectacular Stanley Park.

Things to Do in Vancouver

Plan time on your trip to explore Vancouver, a particularly livable and exciting city. A vibrant mixture of races, a dramatic waterfront setting, and a dynamic arts and business community combine to make Vancouver a particularly memorable port of call. Many of the sights are easily accessible from the port.

Downtown: If you're a cruise ship passenger, most likely your ship will be at Canada Place, right downtown. Within walking distance is much of the city core with almost unlimited shopping and dining.

A few blocks east is Gastown, where the city was first settled, and today an eclectic neighborhood of old warehouses made into restaurants, artist's lofts, condos, and all manner of shops. Do you have a feeling of déjà vu as you walk around Gastown? You may have seen a movie filmed here: Gastown is popular with cinema producers.

Chinatown is a few more blocks to the south (consider a taxi) and its size reflects Vancouver's popularity with Asians. This is the real thing: if you want to eat and don't speak Chinese, make sure someone at the restaurant does! With the waters of Georgia Strait and the North Pacific close at hand, many restaurants feature live tanks from which diners may select their meal.

Visitors and Vancouverites alike are indeed fortunate that its founders set aside the 1,000 or so acres that today is

Stanley Park. It features restaurants, a zoo, the ubiquitous totems, but most of all a stunning waterfront setting right next to downtown. A popular walk leads through the park to a dramatic overlook at Lions Gate Bridge, where all manner of marine traffic can be seen in the tide that pours in and out of Burrard Inlet.

Take the foot ferry around the waterfront. These small craft are inexpensive to take and run regularly from downtown to Granville Island on False Creek, making a number of stops. It's a great way to see the harbor and to get around. Granville Island is a combination of a farmer's and craftsmen's market in a waterfront environment, together with specialty shops and restaurants.

Within walking distance west of Granville Island is the Vancouver Maritime Museum, whose showpiece exhibit is the brave little steamer *St. Roch*. When the Canadian government decided to send the ship and her crew of Royal Canadian Mounted Policemen from Vancouver to Newfoundland via the Northwest Passage, that is, through the arctic ice, it was to be a voyage that made history. They steamed for seven weeks, got frozen into the ice for nine months, and then set out again once the ice freed them. Their long-awaited freedom was short-lived; the ice locked them in again after just three weeks, this time for 10 months!

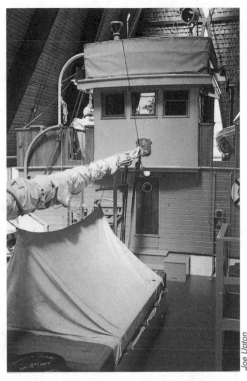

Joe Upton

Preserved near downtown, the St. Roch *once made an epic two-year voyage through the arctic ice pack.*

The Museum of Anthropology

In the early 1900s, collectors made it their business to preserve the hauntingly beautiful, almost mysterious artwork of the coastal tribes of British Columbia. Much of what they found or purchased is housed today in a specially built hall in the Museum of Anthropology at the University of British Columbia. If you have any interest in Northwest Indian art, this is a must stop; their collection rivals any in the world.

Suzanne Billings

What You'll Catch

At most stops in Southeast Alaska, charter boats are available to take parties sportfishing. Typically these boats are modern, comfortable cruisers, able to take parties of up to six. Depending on the season and where the "bite" is, vessels may run up to an hour or more to get on the fish.

Most fishermen like to target on king and silver salmon. Kings, running in size up to 60 pounds and larger, are caught from May through August with the best fishing generally in the first half of the season. Silvers run smaller, typically 6 to 10 pounds, and are available from mid-June through September. Pink salmon are smaller still, 3 to 5 pounds, but run in great numbers, beginning around mid- June.

"Will I catch a fish?" If you just want a king and won't settle for anything less, the answer might be maybe. But especially in July and August when the silver and pink runs are strong, many people easily catch their limit. If for some reason, the salmon aren't running that particular day, many skippers will shift over to target on tasty lingcod, rockfish or halibut, so rarely would you come back empty-handed.

A morning's outing— Alaska's abundant salmon resource means even the inexperienced usually catch fish.

"What if I'm not very experienced?" Don't worry—there are a lot of fish in Alaska, and charter skippers are quick teachers. Many people who have never fished before catch their limit.

"What's it like?" As much as anything else, going out on a charter boat for a day is a chance to get out and see, close and at first hand, some of the most abundant marine life and most dramatic scenery in the world. Whales, dolphins, seals, and eagles are all common sights to the charter fisherman. Bring your camera! Many skippers also throw in a quick and informative harbor tour on the way out to the grounds.

"What do I do with the fish?" In most towns, services are available to freeze, store and ship your fish. Some cruise ships are able to freeze fish as well, and most will happily cook and serve a passenger's fish.

Northwest Artists Gallery

Elton Bennett 1911 - 1974   Detail from The Driftwood Fire

Born in the rough-and-tumble logging town of Cosmopolis on Washington State's rainy ocean coast, Elton Bennett would have had a career in the mills or the woods if he'd listened to his father. Instead he chose the difficult career of an artist, bringing to life powerful images of the woods and the sea that he knew so well.

During much of his career, galleries looked down on Bennett's work. Bennett insisted his art be sold at a price the working man could afford and he made every print himself. Over time his dramatically styled serigraphs attained a popularity achieved by few other contemporary artists. These images planted themselves firmly in the Northwest regional consciousness, standing for the qualities that made life along this coast so unique.

Today the coastal life that Bennett pictures so well has begun to disappear, and his work remains to remind us of the grace and the power of what was before.

Explosion at Ripple Rock

Low water level

West channel

East channel

Shaft: 570 ft.

Raises 300 ft.

Tunnel: 2,400 ft.

SEYMOUR NARROWS

DISCO

205 Race point

Ripple
Rock

Map area

CANADA

UNITED STATES

N

0   Miles   5

Seymour
Narrows

The native village of QUATHIASKI COVE, on the northern side of the channel at **Mile 198**, is the site of the Kwagiulth Museum, many of whose artifacts came from the Christmas Tree Potlatch "bust" of December 1921.

THE BLUFF on the north at **Mile 195** is Cape Mudge; beyond (to the west) is Discovery Passage and the way to the North. The area between Cape Mudge and the Vancouver Island shore has become known as the "Graveyard," due to the violent tide rips that form here when a powerful flood tide meets a strong southerly blowing up the Strait of Georgia.

Gowlland Harbor

Y *PASSAGE* Quathiaski Cove

195
Cape Mudge

Caution
Hazardous tide rips

Campbell River

"UP A PIECE ABOVE VANCOUVER we came to Seymour Narrows. I'd heard about it being a dirty piece of water, so I stayed on deck to study it....There's a sucking whirlpool. I can tell you how it works. It's just like pulling the plug and letting the water run out of the bath tub.
- Martha Mckeown, *The Trail Led North*.

Kwakiutl Country

Blunden Harbor

Queen
Charlotte
Strait

Fort Rupert

290

Alert Bay

B

- Former Indian Village
- Indian Village (1991)

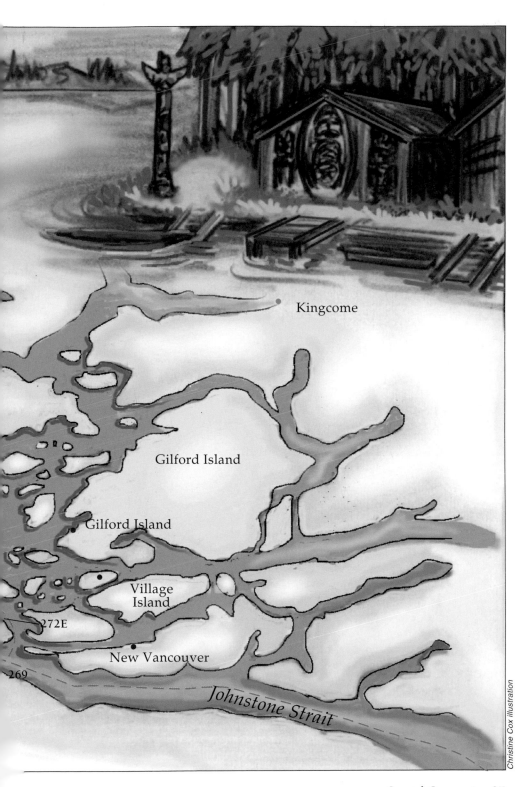

Kingcome

Gilford Island

Gilford Island

Village
Island

272E

New Vancouver

269

Johnstone Strait

Christine Cox illustration

Northwest Artists Gallery

John M. Horton, C.S.M.A., F.C.A.   Detail from Close Quarters

The historic tug *Ivanhoe* tows a log raft into Vancouver Harbor, circa 1910. As she comes up on the Moodyville Mill, she passes a big three-masted sailing ship, deck-loaded with freshly cut lumber and being pushed downstream with the tide by another tug.

Canadian artist John M. Horton is well known for the accurate detail of his historic marine paintings. He lives and paints in Steveston, British Columbia, where as a volunteer he is also active in marine search and rescue.

In May, 2002, the Canadian Forces sent Horton to the Arabian Gulf to record Canada's naval actions in the war on terrorism. His website is www.johnhorton.ca.

Peter Redmayne

Alaska Commercial Fishing

Japanese factory trawler in the Bering Sea, 1975.

Blessed with a rich resource, good management, and some 30,000 miles of coastline, Alaska has the richest fisheries of any state.

The first boom was in salmon, before the turn of the century, when entrepreneurs from California, Oregon, and Washington learned of the tremendous profits to be had off the salmon runs in remote Alaskan rivers. For decades dozens of square-rigged sailing ships left San Francisco every spring, loaded with workers, fishermen, and supplies for the Alaska canneries, to return again in the fall heavily laden with canned salmon.

One of the more remarkable fisheries booms occurred in the mid-1970s and early 1980s, when herds of large king crab roamed the floor of the Bering Sea and North Pacific Ocean around the Aleutian Islands. Using huge pots (up to 7x7x3 feet in size, and weighing 600 pounds empty), a group of remarkably tough vessels and equally tough crews fished this area, infamous for its rotten weather and heavy seas. The money made by top crab boats and crews became part of Northwest legend, but the toll was heavy. Many good vessels and talented crews were lost at sea.

Joe Upton

Hair crab and friend

The most recent boom has been for cod and pollock, particularly in the Bering Sea, using large "factory trawlers".

Today Alaskan fishermen are continually challenged by changing markets, many regulations, and the natural vagaries of wild fish stocks. But generally speaking, thanks to progressive management, they have a strong resource to work with and their industry remains strong.

Morning - a quiet cove, a good sailing breeze making up outside - this is my bell, ringing.

Author's Cruise

JULY 30, OLGA, ORCAS ISLAND, WASHINGTON. "Mom and Dad, I can't believe it—we're in the San Juan Islands and no one knows it's not our boat!" The 11-year-old spoke for all— son, daughter, father, and mother. A neighbor had offered his 41-foot sloop for a week, and when my son spoke we lay off a deserted beach, feeling a warming breeze and watching the seals and the gulls.

"Don't expect much wind," we'd been told.

But oh, didn't we bruise the water today! Taking on any competitors that chanced our way, putting them in our wake, sailing almost onto the beach-front decks of summer houses, then hauling our wind and tacking away. The wind died in late afternoon, and we coasted with the last zephyr into a sleepy cove below the settlement of Olga, on Orcas Island's East Sound.

C&C Redline 41

We rowed ashore to land smells, ice cream for the kids at the little store, and then with friends we drove 10 minutes to a mountain lake and their campsite on a cove with clear, transparent water.

AUGUST 1, OLGA. Coffee on a cloudless morning in a sleepy island cove, with a good sailing breeze making up outside, the family coming awake, and beachcombing, fishing and crabbing ahead. This is my bell, ringing!

AUGUST 2, ROLF COVE, MATIA ISLAND. Slid peacefully in here last evening with the light and the breeze failing. An exquisite, narrow canyon of a cove was revealed in the morning, with sculpted rock walls, a fir and cedar forest, and a few campsites scattered among the trees. The children row along the shore looking at sea anemones, surprising a seal. The morning is still. Beyond the cove, in a mirage above the Strait of Georgia, are the shining towers of Vancouver, British Columbia.

AUGUST 3, FOSSIL BAY, SUCIA ISLANDS. Ashore this morning to walk. Leave the kids playing on the beach. Through the woods to harbors and campsites, but never a car or a house. This is one of the gems of Washington's Marine Park System, purchased by the sailors of Puget Sound and given to the state to manage. No ferry access. The mini-archipelago of islands, harbors, beaches, forests, and campsites seems timeless.

Joe Upton photos

Looking for crabs, Matia Island. Note sculpted rock.

AUGUST 4, REID HARBOR, STUART ISLAND. Another day, another state park. A narrow cove, with yachts moored in tidy lines and tents visible through the trees on its steep sides. Walked a long hour, past a one-room schoolhouse, past saltwater farms, and finally through fir and madrona thickets to Turn Point lighthouse. We look out at Boundary Pass, the Canadian Gulf Islands, and the way North, taken so many times before.

AUGUST 5, SKULL ISLAND ANCHORAGE. For the joy of a good breeze and a strong craft, give me today again! We're off at 1:00 in light airs, the breeze coming on in Spieden and San Juan channels for rail-down sailing, spray flying, the rigging humming tight. At Friday Harbor we tacked bravely right up under the land—and a ferry full of waving passengers—to drop sails and send the crew ashore for groceries. Off again, reaching across to Shaw Island, eating in the cockpit, land, trees, cottages sweeping by. The wind went light and we motored the last miles to Skull Island, where friends came aboard, and we toasted the day, the yacht, and our trip.

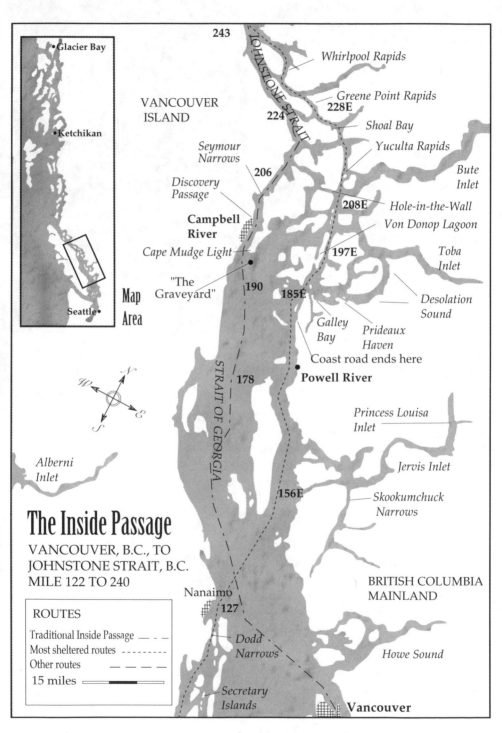

243

Whirlpool Rapids

VANCOUVER
ISLAND

Greene Point Rapids
228E

224

Shoal Bay

*Seymour
Narrows*

Yuculta Rapids

*Discovery
Passage*

206

*Bute
Inlet*

**Campbell
River**

208E

Hole-in-the-Wall

Von Donop Lagoon

Cape Mudge Light

197E

*Toba
Inlet*

"The
Graveyard"

190

185E

*Desolation
Sound*

**Map
Area**

Seattle

*Galley
Bay*

*Prideaux
Haven*

Coast road ends here

178

Powell River

*Princess Louisa
Inlet*

*Alberni
Inlet*

Jervis Inlet

STRAIT OF GEORGIA

156E

*Skookumchuck
Narrows*

The Inside Passage

VANCOUVER, B.C., TO
JOHNSTONE STRAIT, B.C.
MILE 122 TO 240

Nanaimo

127

BRITISH COLUMBIA
MAINLAND

ROUTES

Traditional Inside Passage	— — —
Most sheltered routes	- - - - - - -
Other routes	— — —
15 miles	

*Dodd
Narrows*

Howe Sound

*Secretary
Islands*

Vancouver

Glacier Bay

Ketchikan

JOHNSTONE STRAIT

Map for Johnstone Strait to Cape Calvert on page 56.

CHAPTER 2

Vancouver to Cape Calvert

MILE 93 TO MILE 347

*"Tracing shining ways through fiord and sound, past forests
and waterfalls, islands and mountains and far azure head-
lands, it seems as if surely we must at length reach the very
paradise of the poets, the abode of the blessed."*
                                        —*John Muir*, Travels in Alaska.

Moments in time: Vancouver Harbor, June 13, 1792,
afternoon. Captain George Vancouver in a yawl boat
and Lieutenant Peter Puget in the cutter and their
crews sail slowly eastward, accompanied by 50 natives in
canoes. They are beginning three long seasons of exploring
and charting.

This harbor is the first of many deep and winding inlets
that indent the coastline from Vancouver to Skagway, Alaska,
900 miles to the north. Each has to be explored mile by mile,
lest they miss a narrow entrance that might lead to the
Northwest Passage. These are frustrating trips:

Most explor-
ing was done
in launches.

> "The inlet now took a N.W. by W. direction, without
> any contraction in its width, until about five o'clock in
> the evening, when all our hopes vanished, by finding it
> terminate, as others had done, in swampy lowland pro-
> ducing a few maples and pines, in latitude 50 6', 236 33'."
> —Captain George Vancouver, *A Voyage of Discovery*.

Over the next three summers, the boat parties' hopes will
vanish in many inlets.

Today, cruise ships pass under Lions Gate Bridge (named
for two peaks that seem to guard the harbor entrance) and
enter the Strait of Georgia, which stretches from the cities in

the south to wilderness in the north. To the west across the strait is Vancouver Island.

Look for:

B.C. ferries
S-class, 560'
Spirit of British Columbia,
and *Spirit of Vancouver Island*

B.C. ferries
C-class, 457'
Queen of Cowichan,
Queen of Coquitlam,
Queen of Oak Bay,
Queen of Surrey

- **The milky-colored water** that enters the strait to the south. It is glacial flow from the Fraser River (see P. 28).
- **Log and chip barges**: British Columbia is a legendary producer of forest products. Wood chips are moved in big high-sided barges so full they seem almost submerged.
- **Log booms**: The rectangular rafts of logs towed slowly behind tugs are hard to see at night, because frequently they are marked only by dim and flickering kerosene lamps.
- **Alaska-bound tugs and barges** from Puget Sound, stacked high with container vans, with large items, such as boats, strapped on top.
- **Orcas, or killer whales**: Puget Sound and lower British Columbia, especially Johnstone Strait and the Strait of Georgia, are home to an endangered resident population of these intriguing mammals. Attaining an adult length of 20 feet or more and a weight of three to four tons, these handsome black and white whales are easily recognized by their tall dorsal fins as they travel on the surface. They travel in groups, called pods.
- **Ferries**: The British Columbia coast is served by a large fleet of ferries. Biggest are the 560-foot S-Class vessels such as the *Spirit of British Columbia,* which feature escalators between decks.

The $2.5 Million Herring Set

For a period in the late 1980s, the market for herring was so hot that Japanese buyers were known to fly out to the fishing sites with briefcases full of cash handcuffed to their wrists.

Canadian fisherman Don Dawson hit the jackpot in 1987, with one 970-ton set in Barkley Sound, on the west coast of Vancouver Island, worth $2.5 million. Several other vessels helped transport the catch. When Dawson's boat, the *Snow Cloud,* arrived at the Ocean Fisheries plant in Vancouver, plant officials had a case of champagne waiting.

Holy Hughes

After you clear Vancouver Harbor, point your binoculars south as your ship sails north and you may see boats appearing out of what looks like unbroken shore. This stretch is part of the Gulf Islands (Canadian), which together with the San Juan Islands (American) to the south, form an extremely intricate and sheltered archipelago, containing rural villages, hidden beaches, quiet anchorages—all the elements of great small-boat cruising.

Look to the west for smoke from the saw mill and pulp mill at Nanaimo, **mile 127**. Just south of the mills a channel leads to Dodd Narrows, the narrowest of the passes among the Gulf Islands, heavily used by small craft and subject to swift currents. Smart small-boat skippers heed the admonition from Sailing Directions that "no attempt should be made to pass through against the tidal stream."

I didn't heed this warning—didn't heed it at all—one black fall night, in a 70-footer:

Big bucks: a net full of herring like this (actually 970 tons) was worth 2.5 million bucks to Canadian fisherman Don Dawson in 1987.

> "October 17, 1982, Dodd Narrows, B.C. Went through against a big ebb in the black. Close one! Plus we were towing a gill-netter with engine problems. Fortunately I shortened the tow line before we started through. If I'd known it would be so bad I'd never have started, but once we were in, there was nothing but try and get through, swerving violently back and forth in the current. The guy we were towing had to steer his boat to stay off the rocks. After we got through I called him on the radio.
>
> " 'Oh,' he says, 'That wasn't too bad—except I bit my cigar in half.' "

Joe Upton

Tug Columbia *with two barges of supplies and prefab housing for North Slope oil development, 1975. At night such a barge would display red and green lights, which may be difficult to see. Look for three white lights, displayed vertically on tug, in addition to red and green running lights.*

Be extremely careful of tugs towing poorly lit barges at night

TIPS FOR MARINERS: In Georgia Strait if your barometer drops to 29 inches or lower with a clear sky and you notice a long swell starting from the southwest, expect bad weather in three hours.

SPECIAL PLACES: Along this coast are so many hidden and welcoming nooks and crannies for small craft that it is nearly a disservice to the others to select only a few.

One is Musgrave Landing, tucked into a fold in the hills on the west side of Saltspring Island, 13 miles southwest of **mile 93**. This leafy cove has a path leading up through the woods to a view of the islands and channels to the west. From near here, Miles and Beryl Smeeton set out in their ketch, Tzu Hang, on their way to a rendezvous with a rogue wave near Cape Horn. Pitchpoled (catapulted stern over bow), they survived to write about it in their book, Once is Enough.

Eight miles west of **mile 100** in Trincomali Channel are the Secretary Islands. They offer excellent small-boat gunkholing, smooth rocky shores and a sandy beach between the islands at low tide. (Gunkholing is a small-boat term for nosing around in shallow waters among islands and passages inaccessible to larger craft.)

TIPS FOR MARINERS: Watch at night for vessels displaying three white lights in a vertical line. These are tugs with tows—barges, log rafts, and so forth—more than 600 feet behind them. Watch out especially if you cross behind the tug. Some very large barges or very long rafts may be marked by the dimmest of lights.

Jervis Inlet (east of mile **156E**), like many along the coast here, is like a fjord in Norway. For boaters used to waters where there are roads and houses along the shore, this

Burst wooden penstock at Powell River mill, circa 1920. The pipe burst at night, but workers were able to shut off water flow before mill buildings downstream could be washed away. Generator room filled with wet sand.

BCARS 19925

deep winding canyon is their first real taste of the roadless, unsettled North. Near its head is Princess Louisa Inlet, dramatically scenic, the destination of thousands of small craft each year.

It's worth the trip. Mystery writer Erle Stanley Gardner said:

"There is no use describing that inlet. Perhaps an atheist could view it and remain an atheist, but I doubt it.

"There is a calm tranquility which stretches from the smooth surface of the reflecting water straight up into infinity. The deep calm of eternal silence is only disturbed by the muffled roar of throbbing waterfalls as they plunge down from sheer cliffs.

"There is no scenery in the world that can beat it. Not that I've seen the rest of the world. I don't have to. I've seen Princess Louisa Inlet."

Don't miss Princess Louisa Inlet.

Reached through narrow Malibu Rapids, the inlet is four miles long, with a marine park and dramatic waterfall at its head. (The rapids is one of those places you'll want to traverse at slack water.) Vancouver passed the entrance in a

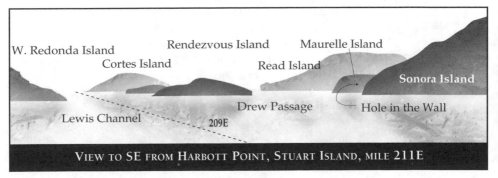

W. Redonda Island — Rendezvous Island — Maurelle Island — Cortes Island — Read Island — Sonora Island — Drew Passage — Hole in the Wall — Lewis Channel — 209E

VIEW TO SE FROM HARBOTT POINT, STUART ISLAND, MILE 211E

Joe Upton

Where the road ends: looking northeast into Desolation Sound from near mile 188E.

small boat, but thought it only a creek. Don't expect a wilderness experience, though; in summer there will be many boats.

Look for the smokestack and mill at Powell River, east of **mile 185**. In 1897, Herbert Carmichael and two other men looking for a site for a paper mill explored the mainland coast from Vancouver to Desolation Sound in a small sailboat; they looked into almost every creek. When they found Powell River falls, with 50,000 horsepower waiting to be dammed and the salt water close at hand, they knew they'd struck pay dirt. The mill they built grew to be the largest paper mill in the world.

Mile 190E to 211E, Desolation Sound: bleak... treeless... shunned by humans? "Our residence here was truly forlorn; an aweful silence pervaded the gloomy forests, whilst animated nature seemed to have deserted the neighboring country."

Many bays here have wild oysters

Vancouver really got it wrong when he named this place Desolation Sound. It was rainy, and he was no doubt discouraged by the number of dead-end inlets he had explored, and his party couldn't find any fish or game. But the place is gorgeous—one of the most popular yacht cruising grounds on the West Coast.

The water is warm enough for swimming. This doesn't happen often in salt water at this latitude—it's unusual north of San Francisco—but a quirk of geography makes tidal currents from both ends of Vancouver Island meet here and create water temperatures higher than any other place on the British Columbia coast. The warmest is in Pendrell Sound, where it's sometimes 78 degrees (25.6 C).

DID YOU KNOW? When railroad lines were being laid across the West, Victoria's businessmen hoped that their city, at the southern tip of Vancouver Island, could get a rail link to the mainland by a series of bridges, including one across Seymour Narrows with a support pier right on Ripple Rock. A more careful survey revealed the impossibility of laying track across the steep mountains around Desolation Sound, and the idea was abandoned.

Look for the steep mountains to the east at about **mile 185.** These dramatic peaks are the ones that dashed Victoria's hope for a railway connection from the mainland. The road along the mainland shore north from Vancouver, jumping the mouths of inlets by ferry, ends for good a few miles south of Desolation Sound. From here, there isn't land level enough to build a road. From here north, it's roadless country; all travel is by boat or floatplane. Not until Prince Rupert, almost 400 miles up the coast, is there a road or a railway connection from inland British Columbia.

The dramatic steep mountains made roadbuilding impossible along the mainland shore north of mile 188E.

Look for aquaculture rafts in protected coves from Desolation Sound to Whirlpool Rapids. They raise salmon and oysters here.

DID YOU KNOW? In the spring of 1949, loggers working near Von Donop Inlet, two miles west of **mile 195E,** witnessed a rare event: an orca giving birth to twins

Gateways to The North.

The land and waterways north of Seymour Narrows and Yuculta Rapids are very different from those to the south. Gone are the frieze of settlements along the shore, the necklace of lights at night. Air and water are cooler, and there are fewer pleasure craft. This is *The North.*

Hole-in-the-Wall, near mile 208E.

No one traveling from the Strait of Georgia north to the cooler and lonelier country beyond can forget these narrow passes where the tide runs like rapids in a river. At the very place where the busy south coast ends and the wilderness begins, nature has set an obstacle, as if to warn the traveler of what lies beyond.

"May 22, 1973, Owen Bay, B.C., four miles southwest of Yuculta Rapids. We lay at the float at this abandoned settlement, our Alaska-bound 32-foot fish boat deeply laden with supplies to build a cabin. Woke deep in the night to odd roaring sound; at first thought another boat had come into the harbor. But it was the tide: billions of gallons of water rushing through Hole-in-the-Wall to the south and Upper and Lower Rapids to the west. Sobering."

Imagine the men of 1897: They left their families behind, borrowed money for supplies, loaded everything aboard ship, and hoped for fortune in the North. Fifteen hours north of Seattle, they crowded the rails to see the dreaded Seymour Narrows. The very air drawing down the gorge was colder, the land distinctly more forbidding. They shivered against the new cold, and for a long moment the chatter stopped and they wondered what lay ahead.

Fur Trader's Language

Words in the Chinook Jargon, a language developed by Northwest Indians and fur traders to communicate with one another:

Boston:*English, white men.*

Chuck:*Water, stream.*

Delait:*Very, or very good.*

Friday:*Shoreward.*

Hi yu:*A great quantity of, plenty of.*

Hootchenoo: *A native liquor.*

Hyas:*Big, very.*

Klosh:*Good.*

Kumtux:*Know, understand.*

Mika:*You, your (singular).*

Poogh:*Shoot, shooting.*

Sagh-a-ya:*How do you do?*

Skookum:*Strong.*

Skookum-house:*Jail.*

Tillicum:*Friend.*

Tola:*Lead (verb).*

Tucktay:*Seaward.*

Tumtum:*Mind, heart.*

Wawa:*Talk (noun or verb).*

From John Muir, *Travels in Alaska*

Seymour Narrows Area Mile 195-208

"The tide, setting to the southward through this con-
fined passage, rushes with such immense impetuosity as
to produce the appearance of falls considerably high."
—Captain George Vancouver, *A Voyage of Discovery*.

This is really worth seeing. Set your alarm, or don't go to
bed if your ship goes through here at night. Start looking for
swirls and current eddies near **mile 193**. Perhaps a third of
the tide in the Strait of Georgia tries to fit within the confines
of Discovery Passage. The current floods from the north here,
and when a big flood is opposed here by a southerly booming
up the strait, small craft better watch out. The locals call this
spot The Graveyard. The steam tug Petrel disappeared here on
a winter night in 1952, overwhelmed by the tide rips so
quickly there wasn't even time for a radio call.

Watch out for
tide rips with
southerly wind
and flooding
tide near Cape
Mudge.

Mile 194, Cape Mudge. Quadra Island settlers had a special present in December 1927, when the Alaska-bound
steamer Northwestern ran ashore loaded with Christmas
goods. The ship was abandoned without loss of life, and the
local people made sure the cargo wasn't wasted. The hardy
old ship was salvaged and put back to work.

Mile 197, Campbell River and Discovery Pier. The big
dock, with flags and banners, was built for sports fishermen
to take advantage of the area's abundant salmon runs.

The village of Quathiaski Cove, on the eastern side of the
channel at **mile 198**, is the site of the Kwagiulth Museum
and its dramatic collection of native art.

Mile 200 to 204: Look for vessels waiting for slack water
along the eastern side of the channel. During the Gold Rush
years, from 1897 to about 1910, settlers on the Quadra Island
shore would sometimes hear sled dogs barking on the ships
waiting for the tide. If conditions allowed, they might row
out for a visit and get the news from up north.

Be sure to be on
deck when you
transit Seymour
Narrows.

Mile 205, Seymour Narrows: "We're going through
there?" There is no other route north (except the ocean) for
ships of any size. This is a famous place. The tidal currents
race through this canyon at speeds up to 15 knots (16.5
miles per hour), and safe passage is possible only at slack
water, a brief period every six hours. It used to be worse.

Before 1958, Ripple Rock, a stone pinnacle beneath the

surface, destroyed a ship a year. Besides the hazard the rock itself presented, its position created whirlpools and eddies strong enough to capsize small boats and shove passenger liners into the rocky shore.

The task of blasting a rock out from beneath some of the most violent tidal rapids on earth delayed efforts until 1943, when work was attempted from a barge held in place with 250-ton anchors. Before the anchor cables parted from the strain, they vibrated so badly as to make work almost impossible. Anchoring the barge to bolts drilled into the shore was no more successful; the bolts sheared off in days from the strain. Next came huge cables across the narrows, but still the barge gyrated in the current and the effort was abandoned.

A decade later, 3,000 feet of vertical and horizontal tunnels were blasted through from Maud Island. Three million pounds of dynamite were loaded into Ripple Rock; and on April 5, 1958, the largest nonnuclear blast in history turned Ripple Rock into Ripple Shoal, deep enough for almost any ship to pass over safely.

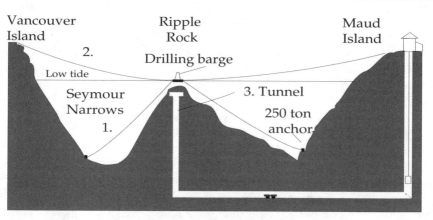

The Struggle to Blast Ripple Rock

1. 1943—Drilling attempted from barge anchored with 250-ton anchors. Soon abandoned—current caused too much motion.

   2. Barge moored with cables to shore; barge motion still too much.

3. 1953—Test drilling reveals feasibility of tunneling under Seymour Narrows from Maud Island. Miners excavate 3600 feet of tunnels and shafts to place almost 3 million pounds of Nitramex 2-H dynamite.

BCARS 19613

Yuculta and Dent Rapids Mile 212E

While these don't have the somber, gloomy, canyonlike aspect of Seymour Narrows, the current, having to find its way among several channels, does some fancy weaving and bobbing, and the whirlpools are the largest on the coast.

This is the route of choice for tugs and log rafts, whose skippers frequently had to shoot Dent Rapids at slack water, then wait in Mermaid Bay for the slack in Yuculta Rapids 12 hours later. According to local lore, traveling whales waited for slack water before traversing these rapids.

TIPS FOR MARINERS: The steamer route north goes directly from Discovery Passage through Seymour Narrows. Small craft, however, use a longer, winding, but more sheltered route (route numbers marked east on chart) via the northern passes: Yuculta Rapids, Cordero Channel, Greene Point Rapids, Wellbore Channel, and Whirlpool Rapids. Most vessels can traverse Greene Point and Whirlpool rapids when the tide is running, but can't do it at Yuculta Rapids.

Consider Vancouver's men in their small and frail sailing ships or rowing up small waterways in longboats, without chart, engine, or tide book. They were seamen of the humblest origins; most could neither read nor write. One wonders what they thought, rowing past these islands, through these channels, wondering if the next bend in the channel would be the entrance to the Northwest Passage or a tidal maelstrom.

Taming Seymour Narrows, Attempt Number 2, circa 1944. Drill barge moored to thick steel cables hung across narrows. Drilling was only possible for a few minutes each slack water. Effort abandoned as too slow and dangerous after nine workers lost from capsized work skiff.

Consider the more sheltered route via Yuculta Rapids.

SPECIAL PLACES: Shoal Bay, mile **222E**, nine miles west of Yuculta Rapids, is a good place to wait for a tide change. A public float and wharf lead ashore to a grassy field, site once of a settlement and lodge.

"June 3, 1981: Shoal Bay, 4:30 a.m. Got up quietly with the first light coming to the wild land all around and walked up the long dock, past the abandoned lodge, the rusting farm machinery.

"Back aboard with everyone still sleeping, I started the big Caterpillar diesel into smoky life, got a coffee, drew in the lines and climbed up to the flying bridge.

"The whistle of the turbo, the rush of the tide, the green smell of the woods, and the rich smell of the sea. The noise, the lights of the crowded southern waters fall behind, and the still and wooded canyons leading north open ahead of us."

Johnstone Strait, which begins at **mile 218**, is the Route 1 of the Inside Passage. Small craft may stay in sheltered channels for a while, but at **mile 242**, they have to emerge from the back channels if they're headed north.

Johnstone Strait travelers: the best sea conditions are usually in the morning.

TIPS FOR MARINERS: *Get an early start!* The wind will come up around midday and really boom in the afternoon; expect northwest or southeast wind as the mountains channel the wind. Take advantage of the tide: stand well out into the channel when the current is with you, go in closer to shore when it's against you.

Look for:

• **The salmon fleet:** (see vessel guide p. 67). You'll see gill-netters and seiners operating in these waters. Many of the fish are headed for the Fraser River, near Vancou-

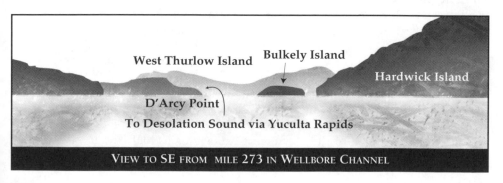

West Thurlow Island Bulkely Island

Hardwick Island

D'Arcy Point

To Desolation Sound via Yuculta Rapids

VIEW TO SE FROM MILE 273 IN WELLBORE CHANNEL

Joe Upton

ver, but some are headed for Puget Sound in United States' waters.

• **Log barges**: In inside waters logs are towed in flat rafts. To make a flat raft, you tie long, straight logs together, perhaps 60 feet long, with short lengths of chain into a rectangular perimeter, which you then fill with parallel rows of logs, strapped or bundled into groups of a half dozen or so. A tug tows the whole works to a sawmill, slowly, as all those logs make for tremendous water resistance. These rafts are O.K. for flat water, but more open waters can get rough enough to break up flat rafts, so Davis rafts were developed, roughly cigar shaped, with thousands of log bundles chained together into a single towable mass. Today, for longer passages across open waters, the logs are moved in self-loading or self-dumping barges. The latter have ballast tanks. At the destination, the tanks on one side are filled, the barge tilts, and the logs slide off into the water.

• **Floating logging camps**: Look into coves where you see logging activity, and you may see one of the floating camps, long a feature of life on the north coast. Whole communities were built on log rafts, sometimes with a store, a school, and gardens, and the camps were towed from place to place as the logging work moved.

Tugs with log booms, near Loughborough Inlet, British Columbia, 1975. The tug's skipper had to work his awkward tow through Yuculta and Dent Rapids to get to the Powell River mill.

Johnstone Strait is prime orca viewing country.

Coastal Companion 55

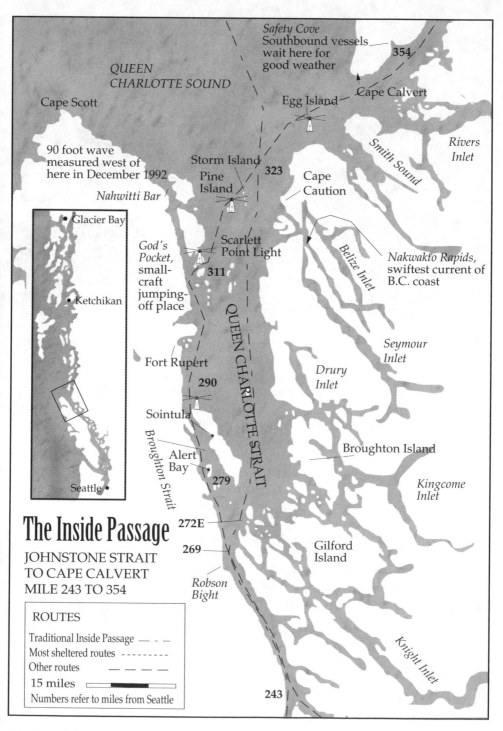

QUEEN
CHARLOTTE SOUND

Safety Cove
Southbound vessels
wait here for
good weather

354

Cape Scott

Cape Calvert

Egg Island

*Rivers
Inlet*

90 foot wave
measured west of
here in December 1992

Storm Island

323

Pine
Island

Cape
Caution

Nahwitti Bar

Glacier Bay

*God's
Pocket,*
small-
craft
jumping-
off place

Scarlett
Point Light

Nakwakto Rapids,
swiftest current of
B.C. coast

311

Ketchikan

QUEEN CHARLOTTE STRAIT

*Seymour
Inlet*

Fort Rupert

*Drury
Inlet*

290

Sointula

Broughton Island

Broughton Strait

Alert
Bay

279

*Kingcome
Inlet*

Seattle

The Inside Passage

JOHNSTONE STRAIT
TO CAPE CALVERT
MILE 243 TO 354

272E

269

Gilford
Island

*Robson
Bight*

Knight Inlet

ROUTES

Traditional Inside Passage — · —
Most sheltered routes - - - - - - - - -
Other routes — — — —
15 miles
Numbers refer to miles from Seattle

243

Belize Inlet

Smith Sound

- **Orcas**: The so-called killer whales (actually, all they're doing is feeding, like the rest of us) are seen frequently from **mile 260** to 270. Before 1964, when the first killer whale was captured near Saturna Island by accident—they had been trying to kill one to use as a sculptor's model—killer whales were thought to be aggressive and dangerous. In captivity, however, the whale they named Moby Doll showed himself to be tame and docile. Unfortunately, injured in the catching, he became sick and died three months later.

Captured B.C. orcas have been sent to aquariums around the world.

Since then, many orcas have been captured and sold to aquariums. The public's exposure to these gentle mammals changed our perception of their manner and intelligence. As a result, Puget Sound has become a sanctuary for orcas, and in British Columbia capturing them has been severely restricted.

DID YOU KNOW? Whale watchers listening with underwater microphones near **mile 235** heard what sounded like killer whales singing the tune, "It's raining, it's pouring." Researchers in other parts of Canada have reported the same experience.

Two miles up the Kingcome River, past the Halliday Ranch, is the Kwakiutl village of Kingcome and the setting for a novel. (Today the name *Kwakiutl* is often rendered in English as *Kwagiulth*)

EDITOR'S CHOICE: *I Heard the Owl Call My Name*, by Margaret Craven, published by Doubleday, is a haunting and

Life in the Remote Inlets

The mainland shore north of Vancouver is a complex of islands and winding inlets. Half a century ago, logging camps, homesteads, Indian villages and small settlements dotted this coast, served by small steamers. Settlers in remote places such as Kingcome Inlet might row for days to the nearest store for supplies and back again.

In December of 1895, for instance, Ernest Halliday decided to row his pregnant wife from their Kingcome Inlet homestead to the nearest doctor, at Comox, south of Seymour Narrows, almost 120 miles away. He couldn't leave their two small children behind, so they all piled into a rowboat, along with their dog and supplies. The trip took 14 days, although much of the time was spent waiting out storms in Indian villages. The baby was fine, but Mrs. Halliday had them at home after that.

Much of Kwakiutl culture was centered near here.

powerful tale of a young Catholic priest working with the Kwakiutl people. Few books describe the mystery and power of native life as well.

"The snow lay thick on the shoulders of the Cedar-man; the limbs of the young spruce bent beneath its weight. He saw the lights of the houses go out, one by one, and the lanterns begin to flicker as the tribe came slowly, single file along the path to the church. How many times had they traveled thus through the mountain passes down from the Bering Sea?

"He went to the door and opened it, and he stepped out into the soft white night, the snow whispering now under the footfalls. For the first time he knew them for what they were, the people of his land and the sheep of his pasture, and he knew how deep was his commitment to them. When the first of the tribe reached the steps, he held out his hand to greet each by name. But first he spoke to himself and he said, 'Yes, my Lord.'"

Orcas like to rub the rocks here.

Latitude is starting to make a difference in the climate once you get north of Seymour narrows. Even though you're only 200 miles north and west of Seattle, the weather is noticeably moister and cloudier.

The wide cove to the south at **mile 264** is Robson Bight, an ecological preserve where orcas come to rub themselves against smooth rocks along the shore in the summer, for reasons not fully understood.

Mile 269 is one of the places where mariners have a choice of routes. The most direct route turns north into Blackney Passage, then northwest into Blackfish Sound and Queen Charlotte Sound. For cruise ships, ferries and the like, for whom a 35-knot southwest breeze is barely a distraction, this is the route of choice.

Did you know?

Early English explorers spoke so often of King George, who had an unusually long reign, that Englishmen came to be known to Natives as "King George men." Most early Americans on the northwest coast hailed from Boston, so Americans came to be known as "Boston Men."

Photo by Edward Dossetter, AMNH 42298

The traditional Inside Passage route is longer, inside the shelter of Hanson, Cormorant, and Malcolm islands, and thence into Goletas Channel and finally Christie Passage, before entering the wide waters of Queen Charlotte Sound. For smaller craft the longer route is a sure thing: stay out of the big water as long as you can.

EDITOR'S CHOICE: *The Curve of Time*, by M. Wylie Blanchet, published by Whitecap Books, is an unusually simple but powerful account of travel along the British Columbia coast in the 1920s and '30s. A widow with five children whose summer home was the 26-foot cruiser *Caprice* (their winter rental was occupied in summers by its owners), Mrs. Blanchet cruised the north coast in the days when yachts were rare. We are fortunate she did. Her account of an age less busy reminds us of the grace in simple lives.

"People-who-live-in-big-houses" was the way natives from the interior referred to coastal tribes. This is the Kwakiutl village at Hope Island, in 1881. Note use of what appear to be sawn planks, only available after the first white-operated sawmills came to the coast.

"They waited until they had each caught a shiner [a small fish easily caught by children]. 'Squeeze them,' finally ordered Jan. They squeezed them.... From the vent of each shiner came a perfectly formed silver baby. They were slim and narrow, not deep and round like their mothers. The second they were put in the water they darted to the bottom, to the weeds and safety. John kept on squeezing his, and his fish went on borning babies just as he had said. But each next baby was more transparent than the last; and they began to look like vague little ghosts with all their inner workings showing through."

Look east from mile 272E: See the narrow channels between the islands. It was here that Blanchet sought out

The Collectors

In a sense, it was fortuitous that collectors such as Franz Boas from the American Museum of Natural History and Johan Jacobsen from the Royal Berlin Ethnological Museum happened along in the late 1800s when the quality and availability of Northwest Indian art were at their peaks. After about 1920, many of the villages experienced the sort of decline witnessed by Blanchet and others, and it is possible much of the art would have been lost.

Those early collectors were tough people. Jacobsen, for example, who bought trunks full of artifacts on the West Coast of Vancouver Island and hired native paddlers to take him by canoe to Victoria, traveled in mid-November over one of the nastiest patches of water on the coast.

AMNH

Ghost masks from Kingcome Inlet, collected by George Hunt, 1901

"We tried to steer away from the wind, but lost control of the canoe. I must confess that this experience did not increase my respect for the local gods as we drifted like a piece of wreckage in a canoe half full of water until about three miles below Hesquiat we were tossed ashore by a thunderous wave, fortunately on a sandy beach, and lay there filled with salt water." —Johan Adrian Jacobsen, *Alaskan Voyage, 1881-1883.*

They also got a lot of art and craftwork. So much disappeared to collectors and museums that decades later, when the Kwakiutls and other tribes wished to set up their own museums, many of the artifacts available to them were inferior to those on display elsewhere. Museums have become aware only recently that pieces in their collections are valuable parts of the tribes' cultural heritage, and some pieces are being returned.

Photo by J.B. Scott. AMNH 32734

deserted Indian villages, to "try to recapture something of a past that will soon be gone forever." We are fortunate she took those trips when she did. Although the decline and abandonment of the Kwakiutl villages had begun, the sites still were mostly intact, and they were rich with dramatic native art.

"We lifted the long bar from the great door of a community house, and stood hesitating to enter. In the old days a chief would have greeted us when we stepped inside—a sea otter robe over his shoulder, his head sprinkled with white bird down, the peace sign. He would have led us across the upper platform between the house posts, down the steps into the center well of the house. Then he would have sung us a little song to let us know we were welcome.

"Sunlight and darkness; heat and cold; in and out we wandered. All the houses were the same size, the same plan, only the house posts distinguished them. Some

George Hunt and wife Francine at Fort Rupert, 1930. Hunt, brought up surrounded by Kwakiutl culture, was responsible for the collection of much of the Kwakiutl art found in museums around the world.

Carved totems and house poles may still be found in village sites in this area.

were without wallboards, some were without roof boards—all were slowly rotting, slowly disintegrating, the remains of a stone age slowly dying."
—M. Wylie Blanchet, *The Curve of Time.*

In retrospect, it seems that Blanchet happened along just when the old houses and totems were being abandoned to nature. Another traveler four or five years later at one of the same villages noted:

"There was not a soul there today. The large totem that I took a photo of a year or two ago is now lying on the ground and the Hoh hoh totem that I photographed last year has now only one wing. So it goes, till at last they rot."
—Beth Hill, *Upcoast Summers.*

GEORGE HUNT—A FOOT IN BOTH WORLDS: Both Jacobsen and Boas relied on George Hunt, an unusual man, to guide them through the intricacies of Kwakiutl culture and the logistics of traveling and collecting in the days when there was little scheduled transportation.

Born in 1854 at Fort Rupert (south of **mile 298**) to an English father and a Tlingit noblewoman (a tribe from northern British Columbia and southern Alaska), Hunt was raised in the Kwakiutl culture. Though not a status member of the Kwakiutl nation, Hunt gained intimate knowledge of the culture thorough marriage:

"Some times while we are sleeping my wife would start up and sing her PExEla (shaman) songs. Then while she stop singing she would talk to the spirit and she

The Potlatch

Potlatches were celebrations given by Kwakiutl and other coastal tribes to celebrate important events. Before the coming of the whites and the establishment of stores, and in particular Hudson's Bay Company trading posts, these were more modest celebrations, with food and craft items given as gifts. The stores and the work afforded by canneries, sawmills, and the like gave rise to potlatches in which chiefs tried to outdo their rivals by their generosity, giving away hundreds of blankets and even at times furniture, canoes and power boats. British Columbia officials, worried that the potlatches were impoverishing the tribes, banned them. The tribes responded by potlatching in more and more remote locations, and finally the ban was repealed in 1951.

RCBM 1889

seems to get answer back. Next time spirit comes to her I will write what she say to it." —*Chiefly Feasts: The Enduring Kwakiutl Potlatch,* edited by Aldona Jonaitis.

First an assistant to passing collectors, Hunt soon became a collector himself, organizing the Kwakiutl display at the 1893 World's Fair in Chicago, with 17 tribesmen demonstrating their crafts. Many Kwakiutl artifacts in the museums of the world were collected by Hunt.

Alert Bay, at **mile 279**, is one of the centers of the Kwakiutl tribe. The town used to be across the channel at the mouth of the Nimpkish River, where the salmon were plentiful. The tribe moved to its present site when the whites opened a cannery there in 1870. The crew of the Maggie Murphy stopped there for gas in the spring of 1938; the town wasn't what they expected:

> "That night we stopped at the Indian village of Alert Bay at the southwest approach to dangerous Queen Charlotte Sound. This village was a distinct disappointment to us, for the Indians were walking the plank main street in business suits, the shops were modern, and there wasn't a tepee in sight. The only touch of native color was a prominent burial ground where each grave was marked with a totem pole, but the poles were just cedar boards on which faces had been painted, rather than carved."

Flour Potlatch, Alert Bay, 1908. Usually given to celebrate an important personal or tribal event, a chief's wealth was shown by his gifts. Hudson's Bay blankets were a favorite gift.

They did, however, get good advice about the next leg of the trip from the guy at the gas dock:

"Remember this one thing. Get across before noon. In the morning the sound is usually calm, but in the afternoon the northwest wind comes up and it gets too bumpy for a little boat out there."

—John Joseph Ryan, *The Maggie Murphy*.

Sointula, on Malcolm Island, north of **mile 282**, is a very different sort of settlement. The island was settled in the early 1900s by the Kalevan Kansa Colonization Company, a Finnish immigrant group seeking to establish an agrarian utopian community. Unfortunately, with few nearby markets for their produce, their dreams died and many moved away. Today Sointula is a tidy village of Finnish farmers and fishermen.

Look for the evidence of winter storms. After **mile 290** the land is much more exposed to the wind because the high mountain ridge of Vancouver Island no longer creates a lee from North Pacific gales. Trees on shore are bent and twisted, conveying a clear sense of the wilder land and seas that lie ahead.

The God's Pocket-Cape Calvert route is the traditional small craft route across Queen Charlotte Sound.

Mile 297: Fort Rupert lies on the south side of the cove. This was Potlatch Central, as the presence of the Hudson's Bay Company trading post allowed natives to purchase potlatch gifts in large quantities.

God's Pocket, **mile 309**: Any afternoon in late May or early June the boats start arriving and keep coming until well after the northern latitude dusk. They are Canadian fish boats bound

Lighthouse Tales

Egg Island, mile 337. Words such as bleak, isolated, and lonely take on new meanings in places like this. Several lighthouse keepers nearly starved when the twice-yearly supply vessel was delayed. Two died fishing for food when supplies were low. Another shot himself from loneliness and desperation.

And then there was the sea: it always seems to have a grudge against Egg Island. After years of breaking windows and washing away outbuildings, it tried for a knockout blow late on the evening of November 2, 1948. Fleeing to higher ground as their home and lighthouse disappeared into a roaring sea, the lighthouse keeper and his family were near dead from hypothermia and lack of food when rescued five days later.

Joe Upton

for the northern fisheries and American salmon seiners and gill-netters. Some are friends who perhaps haven't seen each other since the previous season. The anchorage is small, vessels raft up and the crews visit their neighbors as they put their boats in order, tie down loose gear, and get ready for the trip across.

This small harbor, which is on the west side of Hurst Island in Christie Passage, is the traditional jumping-off place for the 40 breezy miles across Queen Charlotte Sound. On fall evenings the scene is apt to be different. Boats get beat up at that time of year, and the ones that slide in as the early dusk falls might have antennas snapped off, perhaps a window broken.

It is also the site of God's Pocket Resort, established in 1986 after its owners, who were cruising the area by sailboat, noticed its gorgeous location and good fishing. Don't want to cook after a breezy trip across The Queen's Pond? Tie up and stop in for a nice steak or halibut dinner. It wasn't like this in the old days!

TIPS FOR MARINERS: Harbor too full to anchor? Try going across to the narrow gut east of the Lucan Islands. The bottom's hard and a southeast wind will whistle through it, but there's no chop, and it's a lot better than being outside in the windy black.

Seventeen miles west, exposed to the full fury of storms sweeping off the North Pacific, Nahwitti Bar guards the passage to the west coast of Vancouver Island.

Just... how... bad does it get out there? In late November of 1993, the Canadian Coast Guard measured the highest sea

Why they call it God's Pocket - Most Inside Passage travelers have a tale or two about Queen Charlotte Sound. God's Pocket on the south and Safety Cove on the north are the traditional jumping-off places for this breezy 40-mile crossing.

Leave early when crossing Queen Charlotte Sound.

Feared by small craft sailors, the seas in Queen Charlotte Sound hardly affect cruise ships.

ever recorded off the British Columbia coast. Fifty miles west of God's Pocket near Triangle Island, the sea was 93 feet high—nine stories tall.

If you're on a cruise ship, don't worry about that: they stay inside. And besides, in November your cruise ship is in the Caribbean, not the Northwest. But I wouldn't try it in my fish boat.

CROSSING QUEEN CHARLOTTE SOUND: Consider the names along this route: God's Pocket, Storm Islands, Cape Caution, Safety Cove. The worst part about this crossing is it is so exposed to winds from any direction. The tides flowing out of the inlets, the bottom contours, and other features create tide rips far from land. If you are in a small boat, leave early. The fellow at Alert Bay in 1938 who said that had it right: mariners set their alarms for 3 o'clock, get up, sniff the weather, and if "it's a chance," start across. Most who cross Queen Charlotte Sound have stories to tell.

The *Maggie Murphy* boys squeaked across (the wind came up, but not until they were almost at Safety Cove), but they had other problems:

> "Since leaving Tacoma we hadn't managed to warm even a can of soup on our camp stove. Each morning it dribbled gasoline all over its chin, then burst into flames two feet high when the match was applied. This called for vigorous action with the fire extinguisher. When we did succeed in starting it, the contraption would give off almost as many fumes as the engine, but nowhere near as much heat. The stove finally drove us to discovering the only convenient means of cooking on the boat. When the engine was running, we merely placed a can of beans on the exhaust manifold, and within an hour, the meal was piping hot and ready to serve."
> — John Joseph Ryan, *The Maggie Murphy*.

Did you know?

In one particularly bad forest fire season in the British Columbia interior in the early 1970s, so much smoke drifted down to the coast that mariners had to use their radars to pick their way through it.

Traveler's Guide to Work Boats

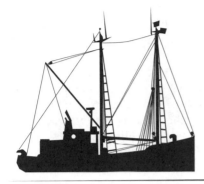

HALIBUT SCHOONER. Size: 60 to 100 feet. Range: Washington coast to Bering Sea. Distinguishing features: Two masts, setting chute, baiting shack on stern. Gear: longline for halibut or black cod. Crew: 5 to 8. History: Some of these fine vessels were built in the 1920s or earlier. They fish by setting strings of baited hooks in deep water. See P. 106.

KING CRABBER. Size: 80 to 160 feet or more. Range: Bering Sea and Aleutian Islands, occasionally in Southeast Alaska. Distinguishing features: articulating cranes for moving pots. Gear: large metal pots (up to 8-by-8-by-3 feet) fished in deep water for king crab. Crew: 4 to 6. History: In the early 1980s some crewmen made $100,000 in a three-month season. Today fewer crab mean harder times.

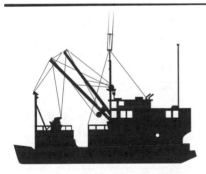

POWER SCOW. Size: 70 to 100 feet. Range: throughout Alaska. Distinguishing features: Boxy shape, pilothouse and living quarters aft, twin booms. Gear: used as salmon tenders. Crew: 3 to 7. History: Many were built for World War II Aleutian Campaign. Popular for their shallow draft and large capacity. One, the *Balaena*, even has room below decks for a salt water hot tub.

PURSE SEINER. Size: 35 to 58 feet. Range: throughout Alaska. Distinguishing features: Round power block hung on boom, carries or tows large skiff. Gear: encircling net. Crew: 3 to 7. History: Used for herring in spring, salmon in summer. Many vessels built to Alaska-limit rule: 58 feet maximum overall length. See page 116.

Traveler's Guide to Work Boats

SALMON TROLLER. Size: 30 to 50 feet. Range: northern California to Yakutat, Alaska. Distinguishing features: tall trolling poles. Gear: lures and baits. Crew: 1 to 2. History: In the 1980s, Alaska established two different troll licenses. Power trollers have mechanical gurdies or winches to raise and lower the lines. Hand trollers, which display HT plaques, must crank lines up and down by hand. See page 75.

SALMON GILL-NETTER. Size: 28 to 45 feet. Range: Columbia River to Bristol Bay, Alaska. Distinguishing features: Net drum or reel mounted in stern with vertical rollers aft. Gear: surface drift gill net, 16 feet deep by 900 to 1,200 feet long. Crew: 1 to 4. History: Many gill-netters bring their families for the season, especially in Southeast Alaska. See page 117.

DRUM SEINER. Size: 50 to 75 feet. Range: Puget Sound to northern British Columbia. Distinguishing features: Large steel drum or reel mounted aft, sometimes recessed; large skiff towed astern or aboard. Gear: encircling net. Crew: 4 to 7. History: Prohibited in Alaska. In British Columbia, fishermen may not have engines in skiff.

SCHOONER-STYLE TENDER (HOUSE AFT). Size: 60 to 100 feet. Range: throughout British Columbia and Alaska. Distinguishing features: Carries no fishing gear; usually displays fish company identifying sign, such as "Icicle Seafoods." Gear: none. Crew: 2 to 5. History: Vessels vary; some date to the 1920s, when they were built to service fish traps (outlawed in 1958).

FLOATER (FLOATING PROCESSOR). Size: 150 to 600 feet. Range: Gulf of Alaska and Bering Sea. Occasionally seen in Southeast Alaska. Distinguishing features: Cluttered superstructures with cranes, housing trailers, and so forth. Sometimes has vessels unloading alongside. Gear: none. Crew: 20 to 200 or more. History: Much Alaska fishing occurs remote from town-based processing plants. Floating processors can move from fishery to fishery.

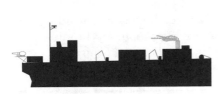

FACTORY TRAWLER. Size: 120 to 400 feet. Range: Bering Sea and Aleutian Islands. Distinguishing features: High sides, large gantry and net reel aft. Gear: trawl nets for cod and pollock. Crew: 20 to 150. History: Before the mid-1980s, foreign factory trawlers dominated the Bering Sea. Today, American-owned vessels have displaced the foreign fleets.

HOUSE-FORWARD TENDER. Size: 50 to 100 feet. Range: throughout Alaska. Distinguishing features: No fishing gear, but has weighing or pumping equipment aboard as well as fish company sign. Gear: none. Crew: 3 to 5. History: During the July peak of the salmon season, hundreds of tenders of all sorts work the waters of Alaska. Look for "CASH" signs, signifying buyers who don't have their own fleets.

HOUSE-AFT CRABBER. Size: 80 to 200 feet. Range: Bering Sea and Aleutians. Occasionally in Southeast Alaska as tenders. Distinguishing features: Tall house aft with deep well deck forward and articulated cranes for handling crab pots. Gear: large metal pots (up to 8-by-8-by-3 feet) fished in deep water for king crab. Crew: 4 to 8 or more. History: Popular design allows skipper to see crew working; evolved from halibut schooners.

Traveler's Guide to Work Boats

TUG. Size: 40 to 150 feet. Range: all waters. Distinguishing features: High bow, low deck aft with tow winch behind deckhouse. Gear: none. Crew: 3 to 8. History: Many supplies arrive in Alaska by barge and tug, especially in Southeast Alaska. During the rush to get pipeline and drilling supplies to Prudhoe Bay in 1975, tugs were chartered from as far away as Louisiana.

SELF-LOADING LOG BARGE. Size: 200 to 400 feet. Range: Puget Sound to Southeast Alaska. Distinguishing features: Twin cranes on tall wide supporting structures. Gear: none. Crew: 2 to 4. History: For long distances or rough water, towing logs in traditional rafts is unsuitable. These barges and their cousin, the self dumping barge (ballast tanks flooded so that logs slide off) are used to reduce losses on these routes.

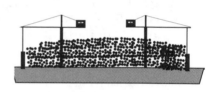

WOOD-CHIP BARGE. Size: 200 to 300 feet. Range: Puget Sound to Southeast Alaska. Distinguishing features: High-sided barges with chips heaped and spilling over, sometimes loaded so that barge is almost awash. Gear: none. Crew: none. History: A generation ago all sawmills had sawdust burners. Today environmental regulations and the demand for chips for paper making and chemical production have changed this waste into a valuable product.

TRACTOR TUG. Size: 100 to 160 feet. Range: Puget Sound. Distinguishing features: Pilothouse is more amidships than other tugs. Gear: none. Crew: 4 to 6. History: This unusual tug doesn't have a propeller. Rotating vertical fins beneath the vessel propel it and allow it to move sideways or turn in its own length. Used frequently for oil tanker escort duty in Puget Sound.

Northwest Artists Gallery

Ray Troll   Fish Worship 1990

There is in Alaska a certain fascination, even magnetism, between fish and man. Nowhere else are their lives so intimately intertwined than in this misty archipelago.

And no one has brought fish and the world beneath the waves more to the forefront of the regional consciousness than Ketchikan artist Ray Troll. At first it was his powerful T-shirt images like this one that won him a growing following. Today, after several major museum and traveling shows of his work, Troll is widely recognized for his unique (some say obsessed) vision.

See for yourself at his SoHo Coho Gallery, upstairs in the Star Building on Ketchikan's Creek Street.

Handlogger's World

Logging the steep fjord walls near
Swanson Bay, mile 460

473

Butedale
Cannery

Graham
Reach

Swanson
Bay

453

Northwest Artists Gallery

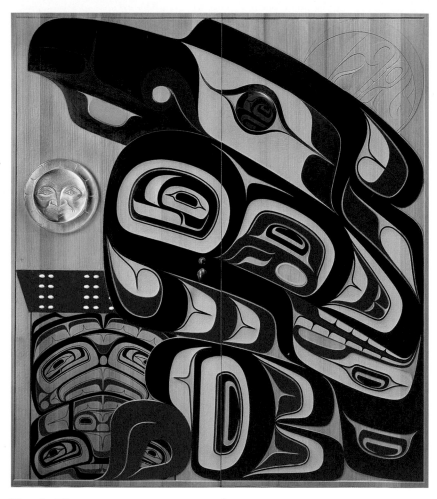

Marvin Oliver

Box of Daylight 1992

This carved and painted door represents Raven, releasing the sun. According to legend, Raven stole the box containing the sun, the moon and the stars, and placed them in the sky.

Marvin Oliver is an internationally recognized contemporary Native American artist. He is best known for combining a variety of materials: bronze, copper, steel, glass, wood and paper. Marvin merges the spirit of past traditions with those of the present, creating a unique and innovative style. His works can be found in private and public collections nationwide, and are on display at the Marvin Oliver Gallery in Seattle and the Alaska Eagle Arts gallery on Creek Street in Ketchikan, Alaska.

Salmon Trolling

More than any other Alaskan fishery, salmon trolling is an art. The fisherman must choose among many styles and colors of lures or bait for the one just right for the particular time of day, depth of water, color of sky, and other factors.

Identified by their tall trolling poles, vertical for traveling, lowered to 45 degrees for fishing, these ubiquitous craft use hooks and lines to catch king, silver, sockeye, chum, and pink salmon. Some of the larger boats are "freezer trollers," able to make longer trips, not limited by how long their ice lasts. Most boats, however, make trips of up to a week and deliver a premium-quality iced fish. Most trollers use small power-operated drums to haul in their lines. Some smaller vessels, displaying "HT" signs, may use only hand power for this task.

Although net-fishing vessels are restricted to certain areas, trollers pretty much have the entire region to choose from when their season is open.

The troller's life is solitary, at times even spiritual. These fishermen, especially those who fish offshore, become much more separated from the cares of the land than their net-fishing brethren.

TROLLER'S DICTIONARY:

BIG SCORE: good catch.

FAIRWEATHER GROUND: popular offshore trolling area northwest of Cape Spencer.

FLASHER: a large (to 12 inches long) rectangular, shiny, metallic device to attract fish.

HOOTCHIE: plastic squid lure, available in many colors.

SKUNK DAY: no fish.

SMILIE: very large king salmon.

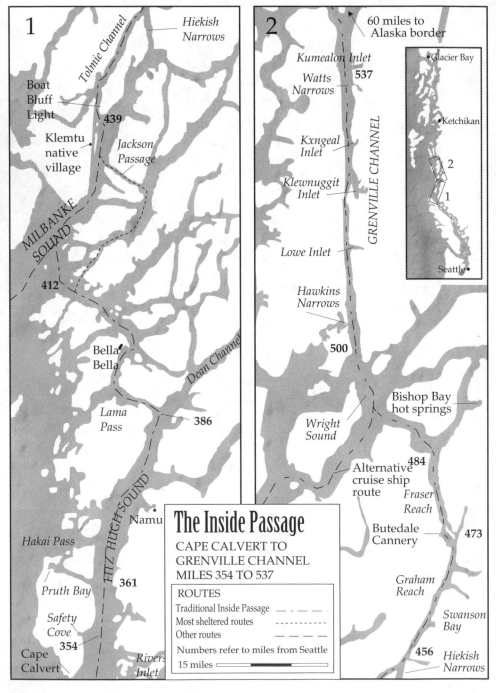

1

Hiekish Narrows

Tolmie Channel

Boat Bluff Light

439

Klemtu native village

Jackson Passage

MILBANKE SOUND

412

Bella Bella

Dean Channel

Lama Pass

386

FITZ HUGH SOUND

Namu

Hakai Pass

Pruth Bay

361

Safety Cove

354

Cape Calvert

Rivers Inlet

2

60 miles to Alaska border

Kumealon Inlet

Watts Narrows

537

Kxngeal Inlet

Klewnuggit Inlet

Lowe Inlet

GRENVILLE CHANNEL

Hawkins Narrows

500

Bishop Bay hot springs

Wright Sound

Alternative cruise ship route

484

Fraser Reach

Butedale Cannery

473

Graham Reach

Swanson Bay

456

Hiekish Narrows

Glacier Bay

Ketchikan

2

1

Seattle

The Inside Passage

CAPE CALVERT TO
GRENVILLE CHANNEL
MILES 354 TO 537

ROUTES

Traditional Inside Passage — · — · —

Most sheltered routes - - - - - - - -

Other routes — — — —

Numbers refer to miles from Seattle

15 miles

CHAPTER 3

Hecate Strait and The Northern Canyons

CAPE CALVERT, MILE 347, TO CHATHAM SOUND, MILE 560

The little steamer, seeming hardly larger than a duck, turning into some passage not visible until the moment of entering it, glided into a wide expanse—a sound filled with islands, sprinkled and clustered in forms and compositions such as nature alone can invent; some of them so small the trees growing on them seem like little handfuls culled from the neighboring woods and set into the water to keep them fresh.
—*John Muir,* Travels in Alaska.

A lthough small craft, smaller cruise ships, and most ferries enter inside waters north of Queen Charlotte Sound, larger cruise ships take one of several alternatives. The straightest is up Hecate Strait, and then into U.S. waters at Dixon Entrance. (The Inside Passage is through narrower channels farther east.) But many cruise ships elect to take a more scenic route, via Laredo and Principe channels. Other routes are through Milbanke Sound, mile 422, or Wright Sound, mile 492. See map on page 78.

Small craft almost always travel north via the Northern Canyons route.

Why do so many cruise ships go up Hecate Strait instead of inside? Because the largest ships are almost 900 feet long, and vessels this long have difficulty making the tighter turns, particularly at Boat Bluff, **mile 439**, or Hiekish Narrows, **mile**

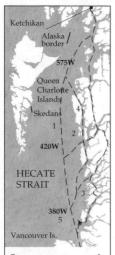

Steamer routes north
of Vancouver Island

1 - Hecate Strait route
2 - Grenville Channel route
3 - Millbanke Sound route
4 - Laredo Sound Route
5 - Inside Passage route

←——— 70 miles ———→

Cruise ships
may take one of
several routes in
this vicinity.

454. Smaller cruise ships can manage these two spots, but they find Lama Pass, and especially the turn at Dryad Point, **mile 400** a little tight; they miss both by taking Milbanke Sound instead.

Distance saved? Actually, it doesn't matter much. The distance from Pine Island to Tree Point (the first lighthouse in Southeast Alaska) is almost exactly the same whether you follow the narrowest passages of the traditional Inside Passage, or go straight up Hecate Strait. We'll look at the Hecate Strait route first.

The Steamer Route via Hecate Strait

The whole east side of Hecate Strait is a maze of islands, channels, and rock piles with hardly any permanent settlements, and is frequented mostly by Canadian salmon trollers.

Look for commercial and sports salmon trollers near **mile 380W** at Hakai Passage. You may also see the larger vessels that carry and house sport fishermen in this area.

Some of the very best fishing requires threading your way, towing hooks and lures, through a maze of underwater peaks and valleys. It is challenging; being off course by 50 feet can mean having your fishing gear torn off on the rocks. The successful fishermen know the shapes of the underwater landscape by heart. When the fish are running, when you're flying the trolling gear just off the walls of some unseen canyon below you, and your poles vibrate with the hits of the big kings—it's an exhilarating experience.

New York writer Edith Iglauer came to this coast when she married Canadian fisherman John Daly in 1974. It was a different life than she had known.

"We trolled back and forth in a half circle, with the sounder plunging to sixty fathoms and leaping up to twenty, then dropping to thirty and then—hold your breath—rising to ten for a single flash before the (engine) roared as John revved up and swiftly moved away from jagged underwater peaks...

"I alternately looked ahead and watched John maneuver in and out among the rocks and pull in fish, in a sunset that threw a glow across the mountains, across the water, across John's face, setting off a fiery gleam from his sunglasses. He...gave me a radiant smile...and grabbed the wheel to turn into the pounding waves.

"I leaned over and shouted, 'Don't you ever get scared?'

" 'I love it!' he shouted back. 'I've been steering this edge for thirty-five years and I love every minute of it!' " —Edith Iglauer, *Fishing With John.*

Look for red flags on poles in the water: they mark the buoys of underwater halibut longlines. Canadian fishermen set miles of these lines along the bottom, with thousands of baited hooks. A good day's catch could be 25,000 pounds or more of these big flounder-like fish, weighing up to 500 pounds apiece.

Some cruise ships swing east at **mile 410W** to rejoin the Inside Passage at Wright Sound, **mile 493.**

All the land to the west from **mile 420W** to **mile 575W** is the Queen Charlotte Islands: five large islands and many smaller ones separated by intricate waterways. They were settled by Haidas, who suffered the same ravages of disease and alcoholism as their coastal brothers. Logging employs most island residents.

Kayakers, campers, and travelers seeking a quieter vacation pace have found it in the Charlottes. Boating guides stress the remoteness of the coast and the importance of carrying adequate survival equipment and leaving a travel plan with a friend ashore.

From 1910 to 1941, a whaling station operated at Rose Inlet, about 35 miles west of **mile 420W**, taking hundreds of the blue, sperm, finback, and humpback whales each year. These boats operated in one of the most rugged parts of the northwest coast, in all sorts of weather, without the navigational electronics we take for granted today.

Coiling halibut longline gear, circa 1920. Each coil contains 1,800 feet of line and perhaps 100 hooks. Tied together into "strings" with a buoy and anchor at each end, vessels typically set and retrieve several miles of gear in a day.

Thirty miles west of **mile 480W** is Skedans, the site of a large Haida village, now abandoned, but with many remaining totems and other artifacts. The Haida watchmen guide visitors who come by boat from Sandspit or Moresby Camp.

Narrow and winding Skidegate Channel, which separates the two largest islands, Graham on the north and Moresby to the south, lies west of **mile 510W**, although the landform shapes make it difficult to see the channel from Hecate Strait.

Southerly gales and large flooding tides may make area near 575W impassable.

At its northern end, at **mile 575W**, Hecate Strait narrows from 50 miles to about 20 miles wide, and shallows to a hundred feet or so. When a heavy southerly gale blowing north up the strait is opposed by a big tide flooding south, breakers will form across the entire channel, as they did for us in a new, steel, king crab vessel in 1971. Our ship looked so big tied to the dock in Seattle, but the farther north we traveled (we were bound for the Bering Sea) the smaller she got.

"It was breaking all the way across the north end of Hecate Strait— I never would have believed it if I hadn't seen it—breaking in eighty feet of water. We were in a brand new 100-foot steel crabber, and we couldn't find a way around those breakers.

"By then it was black and snowing hard and we had to try and pick our way through the rock piles and islands back into the Inside Passage. Except we didn't have a chart. Can you believe that— brand new million-dollar boat, picking her way amongst the rock piles in the black and the snow and the wind, with no chart?"   —*Russell Fulton.*

A Whaler's Tale

One whaler who worked the Queen Charlotte Islands put his experience candidly: "The entire area is a sailor's nightmare, offering unexpected, conditional shelter to the knowing, and anxious, if not disastrous, moments to the ignorant."

"Those damn willies (williwaws, violent winds that sweep down unexpectedly off the mountains) would spring up in the middle of the night and shake you loose. Then we'd have to heave up the anchor, stow the chain, and then steam around in the pitch darkness to find a place out of the wind to try it again. Anthony Island, off the west coast, had good holding ground, but it was only a lee for a southerly wind; if she backed up to the west, we had to get the hell out of there, too." —William Haglund, in *Raincoast Chronicles: Forgotten Villages of the British Columbia Coast*, edited by Howard White.

BCARS

The Northern Canyons

The Inside Passage from Cape Calvert to Chatham Sound

40-foot whale caught in a salmon net at Rivers Inlet, 1901. Note gill-netters equipped with sail and oars.

At Cape Calvert, **mile 347**, the traveler breathes in relief; the wide waters are behind, the mountain walls draw closer, until in places two large ships may hardly pass. For the next 200 miles, almost to the Alaskan border, parts of the Inside Passage are like a river canyon, arrowing through the heart of interior British Columbia.

Look for Safety Cove, to the west at **mile 354**. Many an exhausted mariner has pulled in here to lick his wounds after crossing Queen Charlotte Sound, or waited, sometimes for weeks, for a chance to get across.

Sports fishing, though, is big business. Rivers Inlet Lodge, once a cannery, is served by floatplanes from Vancouver and Campbell River. Small outboards take the place of the sailing gill-netters and fan out across the waterways.

The narrow passage to the west at **mile 361** is Kwakshua Channel, the head of which is Pruth Bay. Before there were guidebooks, the secrets to places like Pruth Bay were handed down by word of mouth from traveler to traveler. Listen:

A trail from the Pruth Bay anchorage leads to a stunning beach.

"It didn't look like anything, you know, just another gloomy anchorage with trees all around. We went ashore and found the path, right where we were told it was. It's not that long, maybe 15 minutes at best, then the trees

Namu, a famous aquarium performer, was captured here in 1965.

got real gnarly and twisted and windblown, and we came out on this beach — God! What a spot! It faces the outside, and Hecate Strait is more like the ocean there. Surf and white sand, and deer and wolf tracks — totally wild and unexpected. We just walked and walked with the surf roaring in our ears. It was one of those places that if someone told you about it, you wouldn't really believe them."

— An Alaskan fisherman.

Today a lodge stands near the Pruth Bay trailhead, and the trail has been widened, but the beach is as wild and dramatic as ever.

One summer morning in 1965, British Columbia salmon fisherman Bill Lechkobit found two killer whales, a bull and a calf, in his net on the east side of Fitz Hugh Sound near Namu Cannery, **mile 374**. The owner of a Seattle aquarium, Ted Griffin, paid the fisherman handsomely for the whale. He built a floating pen and proceeded to tow the larger orca (the calf had

Moments in Time

Rivers Inlet, 15 miles northeast of mile 347. It is July, 1925, a Sunday afternoon at McTavish Cannery. Steam tugs' whistles echo up and down the narrow, steep, 35-mile fjord. From 10 salmon canneries—Inrig, Beaver, Kildala, McTavish, Brunswick, Good Hope, Goose Bay, Provincial, Wadhams, and Rivers Inlet—big steam tugs begin towing long lines of 28- to 30-foot sailboats down the inlet. On each sailing gill-netter, the one- or two-man crew is stowing away the week's grub: hardtack, bacon, coffee, maybe heating up water on a stove made from a cut-down coal-oil can. The tug drops off boats as it travels, some sailors preferring the narrower waters of places like Klaquaek Channel, others preferring wide Fitz Hugh Sound.

Just at the stroke of six p.m. a signal gun is fired from each cannery, and boats start paying out their gill nets, with cedar floats holding the 50-foot-deep nets like walls just below the surface. Many times the rain and the mists would descend like a curtain, and each boat would be alone.

The fish would come as part of a powerful drama played out up and down the coast each summer. The fishermen would watch their cedar floats bob and dance as the incoming salmon drove into the nets below. Each day the fish-buying boat, or *packer*, would come to take the fish, until on Friday night the tugs would corral the fleet for the tow back up the inlet to the cannery.

Today most of the canneries are abandoned, or the canning equipment has been removed, and they serve as storage facilities for nets and gear.

Deadheads

If there is one thing the mariner fears in this country above all others, it might be deadheads. Rocks and collisions can be avoided with careful navigation and electronic aids, but deadheads can be almost invisible. Imagine an 80-foot log, floating vertically and almost totally waterlogged, so that perhaps only three or four inches of it are actually projecting above the surface. It could weigh six or eight tons. At times, where there is a swell, the tip might surface for a few seconds every minute or so. All but the stoutest wood or fiberglass hull could be holed by hitting such an object. (See photo page 124)

escaped before he got there) down the windy waterways to Seattle.

They were lucky. The weather gods smiled, allowing them to cross the wide places without heavy weather that surely would have broken up the pen.

In Seattle, the orca was installed in a pen and named for where he was captured: Namu. He became a celebrity, which fostered a new appreciation for orcas and whales generally.

The former cannery located at Namu, east of **mile 374**, was the fishing center for the central British Columbia coast. Namu is the Indian word for whirlwind, which describes what winter is like here, and why the cannery towed its floats around the corner into Rock Inlet. In the 1930s and 1940s, before unemployment insurance made it easier for fishermen between seasons, the inlet was nicknamed Bachelor Bay, as many unemployed fishermen would winter here in floating cabins.

Vancouver's description of the country his explorers found along the inlets that seemed continually to lead off from the main channel is valid today: "The country they had visited differed in no one respect from the general appearance we had long been accustomed to, nor did anything occur to vary the continual sameness, or chequer the dreary melancholy scene before them." — George Vancouver, *A Voyage of Discovery*.

Near mile 455 Vancouver's party suffered its only fatality: a seaman, who died from eating poisonous mussels.

These feelings are very different from his excitement at the beauty of the Puget Sound region. What a difference 400 miles makes.

In the spring of 1793, when Vancouver and his men were working on their vessels in Hawaii, a Scotsman was headed for the northwest coast from the east, from the interior of Canada. (The western edge of Canada then was around Fort Chipewyan, on the eastern slope of the Rocky Mountains).

This was Alexander Mackenzie and his party of fur traders, who were trying to make the journey to the West Coast and back in a single season. These were tough, tough men. First, they had to paddle up narrower and narrower streams to reach the continental divide, and then down to find the ocean. Canoes capsized, supplies were lost, game was sometimes scarce. When they got to the coast, after a 10-week trip, Vancouver had not only passed, he was 140 miles away at the northern end of Hecate Strait.

It's too bad the two explorers missed each other. They would have had much to say; besides, Mackenzie needed supplies badly. His men were exhausted and out of food, and he could hardly persuade them to get into the canoes and head back.

Channel narrows to ¼ mile near mile 390.

Until it faded, the message Mackenzie painted on a rock at the edge of Dean Channel, 40 miles northeast of **mile 378**, was a monument to a remarkable journey: "Alex Mackenzie from Canada by land 22nd July 1793."

Look for Pointer Rocks Lighthouse, to the west at **mile 386**, marking the entrance to Lama Pass, and some of the sharpest turns in the Inside Passage. Squeezing down to a quarter of a mile at **mile 390**, the pass was a challenge before radar when it was foggy or dark; many vessels elected to anchor and wait for better visibility before proceeding. More than a few scraped their plates along these rocky shores, including the *Mariposa*.

Under the command of Captain Johnny O'Brien, the crack steamer on the Alaska run struck a rock in October, 1915, and settled into shallow water with her upper decks awash. As was frequently the case in those days, with so many steamers traveling north, another vessel, the coaster *Dispatch*, picked the pas-

VIEW TO SE FROM NEAR MILE 401, SEAFORTH CHANNEL

MOHAI

sengers off the beach and took them to Ketchikan. The *Mariposa* was refloated a few weeks later and towed to Seattle for repairs.

Bella Bella, at **mile 398**, is a native village that sprang up on both sides of the channel after the Hudson's Bay Company built Fort McLoughlin here in 1833. The fort was supplied by the *Beaver*, a side paddle-wheeler and the first steam-powered vessel on the northwest coast. Built in London, she sailed to the northwest around Cape Horn rigged as a brig, with her paddle-wheels stowed on deck until she got to Vancouver, where she was rigged for power. In her early days, before coal was discovered on Vancouver Island, she was a wood-burner, so she had a big crew for cutting firewood.

Steamer Mariposa, *ashore in Lama Pass in October, 1915. Such strandings were not uncommon in the days before radar. Passengers were picked up by the next northbound vessel with room, and the ship was refloated, patched up and put back to work.*

Towns that Died

Twenty miles north of mile 386 is the old town of Ocean Falls. Carved out of a wilderness in the industrial fervor that swept the developed world in the early 1900s, a huge complex of concrete buildings was built for Pacific Mill's pulp and paper operation. Thousands of workers lived in tidy rows of frame houses. For a time, the Ocean Falls hotel was the third largest in British Columbia. Today, victim of changing markets, the aging plant is in disrepair, abandoned, and the once-bustling town is home to a handful of caretakers.

To the Bella Bella natives, the *Beaver,* with smoke coming out her stack, four brass cannons, and muskets, cutlasses, and hand grenades in racks around the mainmast, looked pretty impressive. Imagine the surprise of the whites when the natives said they were going to build one.

"Some time after, this rude steamer appeared. She was from twenty to thirty feet long, all in one piece—a large tree hollowed out—resembling the model of our steamer. She was black with painted ports; decked over and her paddles painted red, and Indians under cover to turn them around. The steersman was not seen. She was floated triumphantly, and went at the rate of three miles an hour." —Dunn, *History of the Oregon Territory,* 1844.

The lighthouse at **mile 412** is Ivory Island, whose keepers had an ugly Christmas present in 1982: a high tide and storm waves large enough to smash windows and doors in the keeper's house, besides sweeping away the steel towers for the light and the foghorn. Such weather is why prudent small craft travelers take the alternative route through Jackson Passage (see the map on page 76).

If Milbanke Sound looks rough, consider the alternative route via Jackson Passage.

Look for narrow Sarah Passage near **mile 439**. If you're headed north, go to the starboard (right-hand) side of your vessel, and try to have a view forward. You'll swing almost 90 degrees to port, go for less than a mile then swing almost 90 degrees to starboard at Boat Bluff Light, one of the most picturesque of the trip.

This blind corner wouldn't be a place for two cruise ships to meet. With their bridge-to-bridge radio communications on VHF channel 16, ships call out their positions and intentions in tight quarters, like this: "Cruise ship *Starlight*

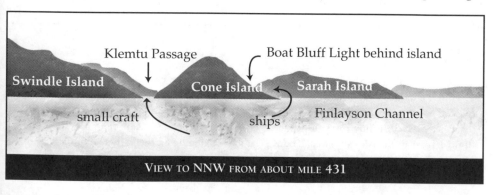

VIEW TO NNW FROM ABOUT MILE 431

UW 12141

Hand loggers—The steep nature of the country in the Fraser Reach-Grenville Channel area made it especially popular with hand loggers, who depended on gravity to get their big trees down into the water.

approaching Sarah Passage northbound. Southbound traffic please advise." Before the widespread use of radios, however, there was a protocol: northbound vessels used Hiekish Narrows, a little farther north at **mile 455**, while southbound traffic came out into wider waters at Sarah Passage.

The northern canyons begin here. The next hundred miles or so are among the most impressive of the whole Inside Passage. The walls of the channels seem to rise vertically in places, and waterfalls tumble down their flanks. In

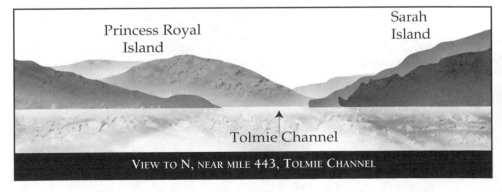

Princess Royal Island

Sarah Island

Tolmie Channel

VIEW TO N, NEAR MILE 443, TOLMIE CHANNEL

places there's not enough room for two large ships to pass. The channel ahead and astern seems to disappear into the hills, and now and again side inlets or channels lead back into the mists.

Unfortunately, most cruise ships can't easily negotiate the turns at Boat Bluff or Hiekish Narrows, and they travel Hecate Strait instead.

This is glorious country on a fair day, but there is another side to this stretch of coast. In spring and fall, when the days are short, the pleasure craft have fled south, and the clouds seem to press down, there is a brooding loneliness to this country that sobers a person.

"Hour after hour we alternated steering with making peanut butter sandwiches while the Maggie Murphy crawled the length of Lama Pass, and Finlayson and Grenville channels, which form a chain of passages through mountains that brood overhead as if they resent every creature that passes through this narrow chink in their rocky backs."

—John Joseph Ryan, *The Maggie Murphy*.

The Raising of the Norseman

Look for steep shores around mile 460. In most places, when boats hit the shore, they stay there. Not here. Consider the million-dollar, 108-foot, steel crab boat *Norseman*. While headed to Alaska in June of 1978, her helmsman snoozed off and she slammed into the eastern side of Graham Reach here. Despite the efforts of her crew and another vessel, she slid down the steep shore and disappeared.

Enter Doug Anderson, diver and salvager. Showing true Alaskan mettle and creativity, earlier he had raised the 65-foot St. Peter from 195 feet of water with used railroad tank cars for buoyancy. Now purchasing a second-hand tug, the *Northern Retriever*, with the profits from the *St. Peter*, he was ready for the *Norseman*.

He found her 400 feet down, perched on a pinnacle. If she slipped off, it was another 600 feet down the slope to the bottom of the canyon.

"It was a hard rigging job," said Anderson who went down with only a wet suit and a special helium-rich gas mixture in his dive tanks. "We had to come straight up with her first, move her out from the bank, pivot until she leveled, then up."

It also took five months, because of the weather and the remoteness of the site. After Anderson and his men got her up, they patched the bow and towed her to Seattle, where she sold quickly for a hefty profit.

Spring 1978

Spring 1979

The Raising of the Norseman

Christine Cox Illustration

"October 23, 1975, Graham Reach, B.C. Ahead and behind the same strip of water between the high hills; never a boat, never a buoy, endlessly the same, hour after hour."

Look for the tall chimney in the trees at Swanson Bay, **mile 461**. It's all that's left of the saw mill and pulp mill that kept the region's hand loggers busy. In the days before chain saws and skidders took over the woods, it was these men, with axes, logging jacks, and their hands, relying on gravity to get the big trees into the water, that fed the mills.

Some of them had no money for power boats. They would row for days to the logging sites and row the logs into rafts once they had gotten them to the water.

This region was especially popular with hand loggers because of the steepness of the slopes, which made it easier for the men, who worked alone or with a single partner, to slide the huge trees down into the water.

"That evening I sat enthralled as they told me of tipping big cedars off the bluffs and into the swirling tides of the Yuculta, of sending tall firs hurtling a thousand feet down the rugged slopes of Knight's Inlet, of the big spruce, which scaled 22,000 board feet, they'd stumped in at Ocean Falls." —W. H. Jackson, *Handloggers*.

Look for the abandoned cannery.

Look for Butedale Cannery on the west side of Fraser Reach at **mile 473**, a traditional stopping place: a day's run from Prince Rupert in the north or Bella Bella in the south. Once a town in itself, with neat rows of houses for administrators and their families and bunk houses for hundreds of workers, it was all powered by water from a lake in the mountains above it. When canning ceased, and only a caretaker remained

Princess Royal Island

British Columbia mainland

Fraser Reach

VIEW TO NW IN FRASIER REACH FROM AROUND MILE 474

Joe Upton

Inside Passage at mile 473, seen from Butedale Lake. Wooden penstock carries water to cannery powerhouse among buildings in center of picture. Look for waterfall just north of cannery.

to run the store and fuel dock, the lights were kept on, to keep a load on the Pelton wheel (a water turbine) generator. For mariners, coming upon it lit up like a city after miles of mono-chrome wilderness, it seemed like a mirage. Then to tie up and find the place occupied by only a caretaker's family was equally startling.

Although several entrepreneurs tried to make something of the place after it was sold by the Canadian Fishing Compa-ny, the graceful settlement slowly deteriorated, until it seemed as if only the stout heart of the Pelton wheel turbine was keeping the place alive. In the mid-1980s the turbine failed, the lights went out, and the place was abandoned to the forest.

A traveler in 1994, though, reported that the Butedale dream was alive again: the Butedale Founders Association had purchased the place and reopened the store and the fuel dock.

"April 18, 1973, Butedale, B.C. I took the traditional Butedale shower in the corner of a vast bunkhouse. There were rows and rows of empty rooms, each with an iron bed, a chair and a bureau. On the walls were a few faded photographs of workers and their girlfriends or families from seasons long past and forgotten.

"This place, out in the middle of nowhere, so big and so empty, casts a spell over me each time I stop."

The Bishop Bay hot springs, 12 miles up Ursula Channel from **mile 488**, is not a resort but a simple, cinder-block, tin-roofed building with a log ramp and a float for moorage. Far from any town, it is busy with yachts in the summertime.

"October 17, 1982, Bishop Bay, B.C. Laid in here this evening southbound after five months in the North. Had no chart; followed friend's advice of 'the second bay on the right.' The country dramatic and steep-sided, but almost gave it up as a poor tip before seeing a tiny handmade float at the very head of the narrow inlet. Almost hidden in the trees was a small low building, with a small wash pool on the outside and the big one, under the roof, on the inside.

"As we sat up to our necks in the hot steaming water, soaking away the cares of a long season, a peaceful rain pittered on the roof, and then an unexpected sound from outside—a pair of humpbacks, blowing and sounding in the deep fjord, many miles from open water."

Look for a confusion, not a profusion, of passages at Wright Sound, around **mile 495**. Four different channels enter here—it's easy to take the wrong one. In the early 1970s, when my wife and I used to ride the Alaska ferries

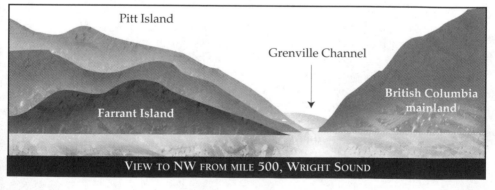

VIEW TO NW FROM MILE 500, WRIGHT SOUND

Soaking away the cares of a long season at the Bishop Bay hot springs. On occasion humpback whales may be seen and heard, right from the comfort of the big hot soaking pool!

Joe Upton

south in the wintertime, we'd play a little game. When we first awoke (we slept in sleeping bags on the sofas in the forward lounge) we'd look around and see who would be the first to be able to tell our position. After many trips up and down the coast, we knew the landscape pretty much by heart, but Wright Sound always stumped us with its look-alike channels leading every which way.

Grenville Channel, starting at around **mile 500**, is where the Inside Passage really gets narrow—down to a quarter-mile. This is probably the route's most spectacular 30 or 40 miles.

"The mountains rise almost perpendicularly, and cause the southeastern section of this narrow channel to appear even narrower than it is. The general effect of so many mountains rising one behind the other renders Grenville Channel one of the most beautiful landscapes on this coast."

—*British Columbia Pilot, Volume II,* Canadian Hydrographic Office, 1969 edition.

If fishing vessels are working in Grenville Channel, cruise ships may take a different route.

If your eyes are sharp, you might be able to pick out the extremely narrow entrances to Hawkins Narrows, to the west at **mile 505**, and Watts Narrows, east at **mile 536**. Each opens to an inlet, the latter a secluded anchorage, the former leading through two other narrows and out toward outside waters.

The house on the southern shore of the Pa-aat River at

Where it gets narrow, Grenville Channel, between mile 500 and 543, offers some of the most scenic passages of the entire coast.

Joe Upton

mile 537 is the first building visible since Butedale, 70 miles to the south. (It's marked *conspic.* on my 1964-edition chart 3772.) The mountains begin to flatten here, and the canyon-like appearance gives way to channels and islands. If the day is very clear, one might glimpse in the distance the snow-capped peaks of Alaska.

"June 4, 1981, Grenville Channel, B.C. In the half light of midnight, a large cruise ship approached us from the north, crowding our 75-foot fish packer closer and closer to the side of the narrow channel. She didn't respond to my radio calls on Channel 16, and finally I just pulled over, until my rigging was brushing the trees, to let her pass.

"Couldn't make out a name, but high in the air above her top deck, brilliantly illuminated, was a huge red flag: the hammer and the sickle.

"The hum of her engines filled the air and then she passed so close as to almost graze us. I looked up, into the plate glass windows of a ballroom, where couples in evening dress peered curiously out at the night, like a scene from Doctor Zhivago."

On a very still evening, a vessel in the anchorage at Kumealon Inlet, **mile 538**, might even hear a train whistle from the Canadian National Railway, winding down the Skeena River canyon toward Prince Rupert, 30 miles to the north. This is only the second penetration of road or rail through the mountains down to salt water since the city of Vancouver, 400 miles to the south.

Joe Upton

It isn't all long hours and little sleep for the fishing fleets—the tire swing comes out on the way north!

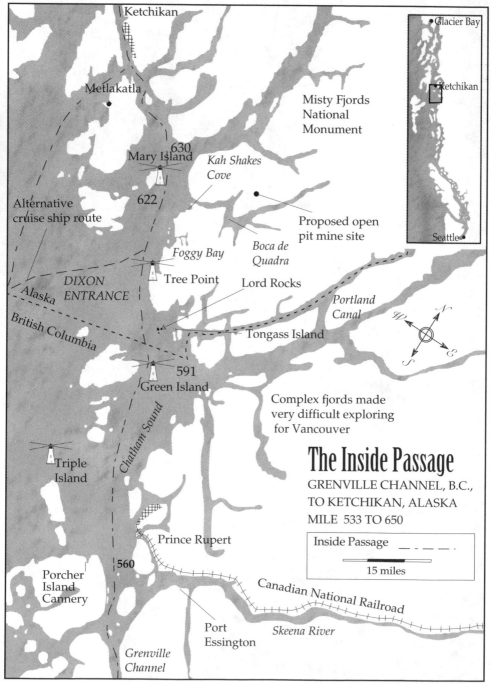

Ketchikan

Glacier Bay

Ketchikan

Seattle

Metlakatla

Misty Fjords
National
Monument

630
Mary Island

Kah Shakes
Cove

622

Proposed open
pit mine site

Alternative
cruise ship route

Foggy Bay

Boca de
Quadra

DIXON
ENTRANCE

Tree Point

Lord Rocks

Alaska

Portland
Canal

British Columbia

Tongass Island

591

Green Island

Complex fjords made
very difficult exploring
for Vancouver

Chatham Sound

N

W

E

S

Triple
Island

The Inside Passage

GRENVILLE CHANNEL, B.C.,
TO KETCHIKAN, ALASKA
MILE 533 TO 650

Inside Passage	– – – –
15 miles	

Prince Rupert

Canadian National Railroad

560

Porcher
Island
Cannery

Port
Essington

Skeena River

Grenville
Channel

CHAPTER 4

The Windy Border Country

CHATHAM SOUND, MILE 560, TO KETCHIKAN, ALASKA, MILE 650

So we came to Alaska, on a wild and lost afternoon, caught in a tide race off a nameless point, in failing light, far from any help. The heavy westerly swell, the dirty southwest chop, and the push of the tide on top made it all I could do just to keep way on the boat, throttling over the big ones and then diving deep into the troughs. The seas came from all directions, and even at dead slow, waves slapped at the windows, sagging-in the thick glass. —Joe Upton, Alaska Blues

L ook for the mouth of the Skeena River, the channel leading off to the north at about **mile 544.** The Skeena is the biggest British Columbia river north of the Fraser; the Canadian National Railway follows it from the interior to the sea. It was the site of five big canneries, including two at Port Essington, 12 miles upriver. Before power came to the gill-net fleet in the 1930s, a large fleet of 28- to 32-foot sailing salmon boats operated here.

Today, because of a decline in the salmon runs and the canneries having moved to nearby Prince Rupert, Port Essington is almost a ghost town.

Two big steamers had trouble along here. First, in March of 1917, the liner Prince Rupert got blown off course in a 70-mile-per-hour gale and drove onto Gann Island, mile 558, so hard that rock pinnacles had to be blasted away before she could be refloated. Then in July 1970, despite two radars, modern charts, and an experienced

Porcher Island Cannery, mile 559, and Larson Bay, mile 553, are good stopping places.

A fish packer tows a line of sailing gill-netters back to a Skeena River cannery, circa 1930.

crew, the 352-foot Alaska State ferry Taku plowed right up into the trees on West Kinahan Island, mile 566, when the bridge officer's attention was distracted momentarily during a midnight watch change. The ship was patched and made it to Seattle under her own power for repairs, but the incident put her out of service right at the peak of the tourist season.

During the Fish War of 1994, Canadian patrol boats waited in this area to capture American fish boats that had not paid a $1,500 transit fee to use the Inside Passage. The fee was imposed as a political move when Canadian officials became frustrated at the reluctance of Alaskans to agree to a treaty allocating fish that swam the border waters between the two countries.

Towns that disappeared: In the teens and 1920s, Anoyx, British Columbia, was a thriving copper mining and smelting community at the head of Observatory Inlet, 60 miles northeast of **mile 588**. Environmental regulations were looser

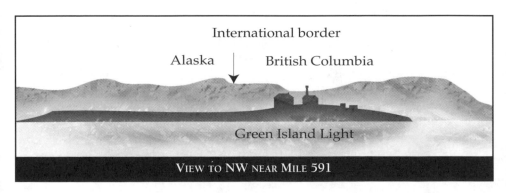

International border

Alaska | British Columbia

Green Island Light

VIEW TO NW NEAR MILE 591

Joe Upton

then; much of the area was defoliated by the fumes. Today the town is abandoned.

Prince Rupert ("Rupert," locally), nine miles northwest from **mile 570** (behind an island, so you can't see the town) is the commercial center for north coast British Columbia.

Look for bulk carriers (freighters) carrying wheat and logs headed to Asia. Alaska bans the export of unprocessed logs to preserve jobs. Canada has no such ban; ships at Prince Rupert load from log booms tied alongside.

Look for Green Island Light, at **mile 591**. According to Donald Graham's *Lights of the Inside Passage,* only the ignorant or the ambitious signed on for this post. Perched on a bleak and treeless islet, the station sometimes resembles ice sculpture after a bitter winter gale has howled down out of Portland Canal.

Study the map carefully here. The three-mile-wide channel between the mountains, which one can see leading northeast from **mile 588**, is Portland Inlet, which leads eventually into narrow, 60-mile-long Portland Canal.

It wasn't easy anywhere for Vancouver's party (except perhaps in winter when they laid up in Hawaii), but this region between Rupert and the United States border was especially difficult. From the British Columbia mainland at Port Simpson, due east from about **mile 595**, it's only about 16 miles as the crow flies to the United States at Cape Fox.

Dusty going in a tide rip near Cape Fox, mile 604.

Exploring the complex channels around the U.S.-Canadian border was a difficult task.

In between, along Work Channel; Khutzeymateen, Portland, Observatory, Nakat, and Fillmore inlets; and Portland Canal, are 350 miles of deep water channels that Vancouver's men had to explore to make sure they didn't miss the Northwest Passage.

Many cruise ships stop to exchange pilots here.

The United States border is at **mile 599**. There are no flags, nor duty free shopping here. The border runs across windy Dixon Entrance, a place where small craft hurry to get across. It's not as far across as Queen Charlotte Sound, but the tidal currents pouring out of all those deep inlets, when opposed by the southwest breeze, can get ugly. The passage, "So we came to Alaska," which opens this chapter, describes a crossing of the tide rips near the border.

Look for the high ridge of snow-covered peaks to the east. They effectively seal off Southeast Alaska from any connection by road or rail to the outside, except in the very north at Haines and Skagway.

TIPS FOR MARINERS: The wooded area behind the beach on the south side of Tongass Island, northeast of **mile 601**, was the site of a Tsimshian village; in 1982, several rotting totems could still be found there.

Many fishermen use the Lincoln Channel route to stay out of exposed waters.

According to one source, people from this village in around 1920 came back to find one of their totems stolen by a Seattle-bound vessel. Incensed, they set out by canoe for Seattle, 600 miles away, and tracked down their pole. They came to a settlement with the thieves but didn't get their pole back; it was eventually erected in downtown Pioneer Square.

The beach in front of the village was the place where they asked for good luck on their hunting and trading voyages by casting necklaces of trading beads into the waters

Tree Point Light

Alaska mainland

VIEW TO SE, NEAR MILE 609

Joe Upton

Lord Islands, east of mile 601: remote, wild, but beautiful. Killer whales have been seen here, almost beaching themselves chasing through the shallows after seal pups for supper.

just after launching their dugout canoes. Beads may still be found in the sand here.

SPECIAL PLACES: Lord Islands, **mile 601**, seem austere and very dramatic. Anchor off and take a skiff in if you have the time. Orcas chase through the shallows between islands, trying to corral seal pups for supper; they have been known nearly to beach themselves here. You might want to either leave someone on your anchored boat or bring a handheld radio ashore with you. It's a rocky, exposed anchorage and the tide runs hard.

Look for salmon gill-netters, typically fishing Sunday noon through Wednesday noon. If the weather is calm, you may also see fish packers (they're larger) making their rounds among the fleet, buying fish. Many vessels remain the summer here, remote from any town or cannery, getting water, groceries, fuel, and supplies from the tenders, or fish packers, that service the fleet. The nets they use here are 1,800 feet long by 30 feet deep; a good day might be 2,000 pounds of red salmon or 5,000 pounds of pink salmon.

The area around mile 607 has a major salmon gillnet fishery.

Tree Point Light at **mile 607** is the first in Alaskan waters. Before it was automated in the 1970s, the crews lived in four beautifully crafted houses set in the woods near the cove south of the light. One house was barged to Ketchikan after the families left.

The southernmost part of Alaska is part of the Misty Fjords National Monument, the centerpiece of which is the canyonlike Boca de Quadra area, to the east at **mile 625**. Also dramatically beautiful are Rudyerd Bay and Walker Cove, 30 miles farther north.

The Boca is 50 miles of steep-sided fjords and side chan-

A huge open pit mine was planned for the Misty Fjords National Monument.

nels, whose sides quickly rise to two and three thousand-foot peaks. Aside from the ubiquitous cannery ruins on the shore of Mink Bay, the land is wilderness, visited mostly in summer by people seeking its natural beauty and in winter by shrimp and crab fishermen.

The Boca was also the proposed site for the largest open pit molybdenum mine in the world.

"Here?" you ask, "here in this gorgeous National Monument, an open pit mine?"

The same question was asked by hundreds of fishermen who were concerned about the effects of toxic mine tailings on nearby salmon and crab stocks.

In the late 1970s, when Southeast Alaska's two key industries, forest products and fishing, were in a cyclic downturn, the mine promised employment to the region. Eventually, to the astonishment of most of its opponents, it received all the necessary permits for construction.

Then, to the surprise of almost all, the project faded away without being built, the victim, apparently, of low worldwide demand. (Molybdenum is a key ingredient in steel alloys, particularly those used in aircraft and missile parts.) Today, all that is left of the grand plans so widely proclaimed is a dock on Smeaton Bay and a road that is slowly being taken over by the forest.

The two-mile-wide channel extending to the northeast at around **mile 630** is Behm Canal, named by Vancouver and charted by his small-boat crews, rowing into and out of each

Cash Buyers

When I was an 18-year-old engineer on a fish-buying vessel, one of my jobs was watching out for cash buyers. Our fishermen, like many, owed money to the cannery for nets, food and so forth, a debt that was repaid during the salmon season.

Cash buyers, working for canneries or freezer plants without their own loyal fleets, would cruise the grounds, paying cash, giving out free beer to those who sold them fish and asking no questions about who owed what to the cannery. If one of our fishermen had a particularly good catch and happened to be near a cash buyer, and we weren't around, it would be to his advantage to sell part of his catch for cash and the rest to us.

So our tactic would be to always anchor in the same cove as the cash buyers, or otherwise position our vessel so our fishermen couldn't deliver their fish to a cash buyer without our seeing them.

Joe Upton

inlet and bay. Halfway up the canal he remarked at a rock that from a distance looked like the sail of a ship. "On the base of this singular rock, which, from its resemblance to the lighthouse rock off Plymouth, I called the New Eddystone [Rock], we stopped to breakfast, and whilst were thus engaged, three small canoes, with about a dozen of the natives, landed and approached us unarmed, and with the utmost good humor, accepted such presents as were offered to them."—George Vancouver, *A Voyage of Discovery.*

The large island to the west, from **mile 628** to **mile 645,** is Annette Island, a reservation for the Tsimshian tribe. Most of the Tsimshians lived in Canada, up a channel across from Prince Rupert, where the village of Metlakatla thrived under the supervision of a Mr. William Duncan. A dispute with authorities in 1887 led Mr. Duncan, along with most of the tribe, to move across to Annette Island in the United States, where they rebuilt their village, also called Metlakatla.

Today Metlakatla, supported by its own sawmill and salmon cannery, is a tidy and successful native community. It was to this cannery that I came as a lad of 19, engineer aboard a fish-packing vessel.

West and north of Behm Canal, starting at **mile 630,** the

Gill-netters partici-pate in a dramatic short herring fishery each spring at Kah Shakes Cove near mile 615.

Tsimshian Indians set-tled Annette Island.

Joe Upton

The area around mile 605 is an active gill-net area. Look for larger vessels (packers or tenders) unloading smaller gill-netters.

land so penetrated by long, deep inlets is Revillagigedo Island ("Re-VEE-a gi-gay-do," known locally as Revilla). For the most part roadless wilderness, it is heavily logged in places close to the shore. Spread along the eastern shore of Tongass Narrows is the city of Ketchikan, beginning at Mountain Point, **mile 645**.

Before the Ketchikan airport was built across from town on Gravina Island in the 1970s, travelers flew in and out of Ketchikan in converted navy patrol bombers, PBYs. They took off from Tongass Narrows in front of Ketchikan, flew 20 miles to Annette Island, lowered their wheels and landed at the airport to meet their connections. (The new airport was a big earthmoving job; look at it carefully when you go by.)

The PBYs had seen a lot of miles before they were converted; the seams leaked. When the pilot applied full throttle for takeoff, passengers might see water running down the aisle to the back of the airplane.

The big cannery at mile 649 operates around the clock during the peak of the salmon run in July and August.

Look for the big salmon cannery just south of town at **mile 649**. The largest boats are tenders, mother ships to the smaller purse seiners and gill-netters. The big containers, or vans, stacked on the dock are full of frozen or canned salmon.

Before Southeast Alaska had weekly barge service from Seattle, people like Captain Niels Thomsen, who had a small freight boat running regularly from Seattle to Ketchikan and other Alaskan towns, kept groceries on the store shelves.

Joe Upton

Abandoned boat house at Tree Point Light, 1982

Thomsen started his business on a shoestring with the help of Ketchikan investors.

"Most of my stockholders lived by Mountain Point, and I really wanted to impress them, so I'd made a dummy radar antenna out of wood, with a pipe coming down into the pilothouse. Every time I came past Mountain Point, I had my son cranking on that pipe to make the antenna go around. This was back in the early 1950s when radar was really expensive. "Boy," those guys must have thought, "Radar! Well, old Cap Thomsen must really be doing well."

—Capt. Niels Thomsen

Halibut Longlining

A traditional halibut schooner.

Iron men in wooden ships were the mainstays of the halibut fishery. For generations, Norwegian-descent fishermen set out from northwest ports in graceful halibut schooners (see page 67) for long trips, sometimes almost to Siberia. Baiting and hand coiling miles of gear set out along the bottom, hauling it back, and cleaning the fish as they came aboard made for 18- and 20-hour days on deck. The stamina of these men was legendary along the waterfront.

Today, the joke in the fishing business is that "all you need to be a halibut fisherman is a few free weekends." By 1994 the halibut season had been reduced to a few 12- to 48-hour "openings," or periods vessels were allowed to fish. This wasn't because of a shortage of fish, but rather that a huge fleet was taking the quota.

It was a poor system. The catch, coming all at once, overwhelmed processors, and gear tangled on the grounds. Finally in 1995, fishermen were given quota shares according to their catch history, and were allowed to fish whenever it was convenient for them.

The northwest halibut resource is strong. On occasion, during a 24-hour or 48-hour opening, vessels have caught more than 50,000 pounds. Prices fluctuate, but halibut has fetched a good price in recent years. Several species of cod are also targeted by longline fishermen.

LONGLINER'S DICTIONARY:

BECKET: a short piece of line knotted into the ground line, into which the gangion is attached.

CHICKEN: small halibut.

CIRCLE HOOK: efficient style introduced in 1980s.

FREEZER LONGLINER: vessel with automated longline system for fishing and freezing cod.

GANGION (pronounced ganyon): leader between ground line and hook.

SKATE: unit of longline gear, usually 300 fathoms long (1,800 feet) with hooks every 21 feet.

SNAP GEAR: system using friction snaps to attach leaders to ground line.

STRING: 10 skates tied end to end, with anchors and buoys at either end.

WHALE: very large halibut.

Northwest Artists Gallery

Rie Muñoz

Whaling Camp, 1983

"A beluga whale has just been spotted and pandemonium breaks out. The villagers rush to the boats, taking oil, gas, floats, rifles, and outboard motors. This is another scene from the whaling camp at Sigik."

Juneau artist Rie Muñoz's cheerful watercolors are perhaps the most widely distributed Alaskan images from any contemporary artist. For some 40 years, she has been traveling the state, to the most rural and remote areas, to gather ideas for her remarkable pieces. Whaling Camp, like much of her work, celebrates village or native life.

Available from fine art galleries or Rie Muñoz Ltd., 2101 N. Jordan Ave., Juneau, Alaska, 99801.

6 Three mile hike to top of Deer Mountain for great views, starts south of Creek Street.

CRUISE SHIP DOCK

1

N

S

Russ Burtner Illustration

Ketchikan

1 Downtown shopping: Many unusual stores are within an easy walk of the cruise ship docks.

Outside of Town: Totem Bight State Historical Park (10 miles N): 14 totem poles, as well as a copy of a traditional clan house, overlooking Tongass Narrows. Saxman Native Village (2.5 miles S): Founded in the late 1800s, this Tlingit village today celebrates its traditions with potlatches, workshops in native art, and other cultural

5 Creek Street Historical District, "where the men and the fish came to Spawn."

4 Totem Heritage Center: In a dramatic setting stand a collection of older totems, without the bright color and sharply chiseled features of the newer "recarves." Worth seeing; these totems have unusual power and drama.

3 Thomas Basin boat harbor: See if you can identify the different vessel types: trollers, gill-netters, packers, and seiners.

2 U.S. Forest Service visitors center.
   Also in downtown: Tongass Historical Museum: Good exhibits of fishing, logging, and early Ketchikan.

events. Wards Cove pulp mill (8 miles N): INDUSTRY with capital letters, this is the engine that drove the economy of lower Southeast Alaska for almost four decades. Logs arrive in floating rafts and are processed into pulp for paper and industrial uses, and also into lumber.

Joe Upton

An Otter floatplane: the biggest single-engine aircraft used on floats in Alaska.

Ketchikan

A Saturday afternoon in summer, 1951. The steam whistle at The Great Atlantic and Pacific Tea Company's Sunny Point salmon cannery echoes across Tongass Narrows as hundreds of workers stretch their tired muscles, start to clean up, and fan out to the bars and eateries that line the waterfront. Out in the channel floatplanes start to land, big twin-engine converted PBYs, and the slow, lumbering Beavers, bringing in loggers from Prince of Wales Island and Tsimshian Indians from the village of Metlakatla. As the sun slants toward the northwest, the fish boats begin arriving from the outer districts, Dixon Entrance in the south and Clarence Strait to the north: big 60- and 80-footers loaded with salmon for canning and fishermen in for a night on the town.

At Big Dolly Arthur's and the other brothels along the boardwalk at Creek Street, the ladies finish their makeup and wait for their first customers. At the police station downtown, the boys in blue check their nightsticks and their pistols before heading out; Saturday night is always busy.

Pennock Island residents (just across the channel from Ketchikan) do their town errands by outboard.

Half a century later, Ketchikan is still *ALASKA* in capital letters: all the rough-and-tumble elements that make this region what it is still ebb and flow through the streets and harbors of this town.

Second largest of only nine towns in an area larger than many states, Ketchikan is the economic center of lower Southeast Alaska. A narrow strip of a town along the steep western side of Revillagigedo Island (locally: Ruh-VIL-lah), its few miles of roads aren't connected to anywhere else.

FISHING: If catching a salmon is high on your list of things to do on your Alaska cruise, Ketchikan might be a good bet. Strong hatchery silver and abundant pink and king salmon runs make for great fishing. If you really want to go after those big halibut, probably Sitka, being right on the ocean would be better.

Two active canneries and several fish processors are busy during the salmon season.

WHAT TO DO: The historical sights celebrate, in some fashion, Tsimshian and Tlingit culture, logging, or fishing. Recommendations: At the minimum, take the walking tour around downtown, and make the trip to one of the totem centers. The Creek Street Historical District, the Tongass Historical Museum, and the Thomas Basin boat harbor, as well as good shopping, are all within an easy walk of each other.

A particularly dramatic hike is up the Deer Mountain Trail that starts just a mile from downtown. At the top of the three-mile ascent is a dramatic view of the waterways and islands around Ketchikan.

SAM'S TOUR: "I always go fishing when I get to Ketchikan, after all, it is the salmon capital of the world. Ask the skipper to throw in a quick waterfront tour if he's got the time. It gets cold out on the water, so afterward I'll stop at the Sourdough Bar for a warmer-upper and inspect the wicked collection of local shipwreck photos. What'll I do with my fish? Get it smoked, lox style, at Silver Lining Seafoods, and shipped home after I get back."

Herring fishermen near Misty Fjords, south of Ketchikan.

Joe Upton

Northwest Artists Gallery

Nancy Stonington

Detail from Cloudscapes

In the fjord country of Prince William Sound, the low-lying clouds lift for a moment, revealing the dramatic high and glaciated mountains that ring the sound.

Each year artist Nancy Stonington divides her time between Alaska and Idaho, with stops up and down the northwest coast in between. Her particularly realistic watercolors of the northwest scene have become a regular presence in this region's homes and galleries.

Nancy's and other northwest artists' work is available at the Stonington Gallery in downtown Seattle, and galleries throughout Alaska.

Alaska History Time Line

30,000 B.C.   Migratory hunters from Asia move across the land bridge from Siberia to Alaska, spread, and settle North America. They evolve into three main groups: Aleuts, Eskimos, and Indians.

8,000 B.C.   As the Ice Age ends, the rising ocean covers the land bridge. An ice bridge forms. Migration slows.

1741   Vitus Bering and Aleksei Chirikov land in Alaska on an expedition from Russia and bring back 800 sea otter skins. Bering is lost on the return trip. The fur traders—*promyshlenniki*—begin outfitting trading expeditions, and the rush is on.

1778   British Captain James Cook explores the Alaskan coast, seeking a Northwest Passage to the Atlantic.

1791-5   British Captain George Vancouver with two ships explores and charts the Northwest Coast exhaustively but finds no Northwest Passage.

1799   Aleksandr Baranov consolidates Russian possession of Alaska with a fort and trading base at Sitka.

1867   Secretary of State William Seward buys Alaska from Czarist Russia for 2 cents an acre: $7.2 million. The fur resource has been used up. Purchase is hailed as "Seward's Folly."

1879   Naturalist John Muir canoes throughout Southeast Alaska and discovers Glacier Bay. (When Vancouver had passed through there was no bay; it was full of ice.) Muir's reports inaugurate tourism to the territory.

1896-1900   Gold strike on a Yukon River tributary brings 100,000 people to Alaska and the Yukon Territory.

1922   Roy Jones makes the first floatplane flight up the Inside Passage; small aircraft revolutionize travel in the bush.

1925   A 674-mile dogsled relay brings diphtheria vaccine to Nome.

1942   Japan invades the Aleutian Islands. The Alaska Highway project is begun to move defense supplies.

1959   Alaska becomes the 49th state.

1964   Good Friday earthquake.

1968   10 billion barrels of oil are discovered at Prudhoe Bay.

1977   First oil flows through an 800-mile engineering feat, the Alaska Pipeline.

1980   Alaska National Interest Lands and Conservation Act (ANILCA) is passed, establishing new parks and settling Alaska Native land claims.

1989   Tanker *Exxon Valdez* rams Bligh Reef, Prince William Sound, creating a massive oil spill and years of work for hundreds of lawyers.

Haida village of Skidegate, in the Queen Charlotte Islands, circa 1881.

Totems

One fair July day in 1981, when I was a young fish buyer waiting for our boats to come in, my wife and I rowed ashore to the long-abandoned site of a Tsimshian village near the southern border of Alaska. Mary Lou searched the fine white sand for glass trading beads, and I poked through the nearly impenetrable devil's club and undergrowth for the remains of the village.

The beach yielded a dozen exquisite glass beads, some little larger than the grains of sand that hid them, yet all of bright color, little faded with the passing of centuries. In the forest was a single totem base, decayed, its grain raised into ridges from the wind and the rain.

A century earlier, Tongass would have been typical of many dozens of villages up and down the coast. On a sandy beach in a sheltered cove, high-prowed canoes would be drawn up below the simple cedar plank-and-beam houses. In front, inside, and as parts of the houses would be art: carved cedar in its many forms, the most striking of which were the totems.

Detail from totem on Shakes Island, Wrangell, Alaska.

Totems were a dramatically visible sign of the success and wealth of the native cultures that evolved along the coast, whether Haida, Kwakiutl, Tlingit, or Tsimshian. Sheltered by a benevolent forest, blessed with a food-filled sea, the tribes could afford the luxury of permanent village sites and ornamental art. Their art celebrated legends, events, or simply the wealth and crest of the family for whom it was carved. The poles were neither worshipped nor had any religious significance. They were records of the past in a society where there was no written language.

At first, the coming of the whites was the catalyst for a burst of creative energy among northwest tribes. Steel tools, and the cash from the fur trade and native employment, led to an affluence celebrated in larger potlatches (see page 62), more carvings, and totems.

By the second half of the 19th century, the situation had changed dramatically. A series of epidemics ravaged the coast, and missionaries and government alike worked to reform a way of life they viewed as pagan or, at the very least, against the spirit of modern commerce.

At the beginning of the 20th century, travelers remarked on the curious combination of the presence of dramatic and sophisticated carved art and its apparent abandonment. The reason was simple: so many natives had died that whole villages were abandoned.

Totem next to Monster House, Masset, Queen Charlotte Islands.

The result was that much native art disappeared, either rotted into the forest, purchased by individuals, or, fortunately for us, collected by museums. But in many villages, particularly on the Queen Charlotte Islands, where the people struggled with the poverty and alcoholism, the tradition of art, as it was practiced in the 19th century, essentially disappeared.

Fortunately the 1960s and '70s brought a rekindling of the flame of carved art among northwest coastal tribes. Today, dramatic newly carved totems fetch high prices and are in demand from Disney World to corporate offices.

Totems have become cultural icons for the Northwest Coast. We shouldn't forget what they were carved to celebrate: the centuries-old success of a native culture that suffered badly with the coming of the whites.

The end of a set; hauling the bag aboard.

Purse Seining

Each spring thousands of college-age young men walk the docks of Puget Sound ports seeking their ideal summer job—a crew job on an Alaska-bound purse seiner. The lucky ones begin work in late May or early June—painting and readying the graceful 58-footers, overhauling and building their expensive nets, and sailing north.

Seining is a complicated operation requiring coordination between the seiner, the large skiff, and a four- or five-man crew.

"Let 'er go!" cries the skipper and the crew pulls the pin on a shackle, releasing the skiff, which begins towing the net off the seiner's stern. The seiner then makes a wide curving turn, typically "hooking" the net off a point, to catch fish traveling with the tide.

At the appropriate time the skiff will circle back, passing the end of the net to the larger vessel. Next the crew winches in both ends of the purse line, pulling up the net's bottom and transforming it into a sort of basket from which there is no escape. As the net is hauled aboard with the power block, the basket becomes smaller, until the fish can be easily dipped aboard.

In the late 1980s, when fish prices were booming, a crewman might make $5,000 to $10,000 in a good season on a top boat.

Salmon purse seiners catch primarily pink and chum salmon.

A broom displayed in the rigging means a 100,000 fish-plus season, a good catch.

PURSE SEINER'S DICTIONARY:

BUNT: the end of the net where the fish become concentrated.

HUNG UP: net hung on object or snagged on bottom.

MONEY FISH: sockeye salmon, much more valuable than pink salmon.

POWER BLOCK: hydraulically operated, boom-mounted pulley or sheave which pulls the net from the water, to stack on deck. Revolutionized seining.

WATER HAUL: a no-fish set.

Joe Upton

Salmon Gill-netting

Made of very fine nylon, gill-nets must be repaired frequently.

Imagine taking your family commercial fishing in Alaska in a nicely fitted out 40-footer—gill-netting three or four days a week and having the rest to explore, sports-fish, beach-comb, and so forth. This is what many men do, fishing the simplest of nets—a floating vertical wall whose meshes are sized to snag just behind the gills of traveling fish. A gill-netter will roll the net off his drum into the water in a likely spot, wait for a few minutes to several hours, and then wind it back onto the drum, standing in the stern and stopping the drum to "pick" fish as they appear.

Although the gear looks simple, fishing it in the tides of the region is tricky. The best fishermen know where to set their nets at each stage of the tide.

To fish for salmon commercially in Alaska you must buy a "limited entry permit" from someone who wants to leave the fishery. Permit prices fluctuate with the prosperity of the fishery and the price of fish. During the boom years of the late 1980s, when the Japanese economy was red hot, permit prices rose to over $400,000 for the most lucrative fisheries. Today farmed salmon has wreaked havoc with wild salmon prices and most permits sell for less than a quarter of what they did at the peak.

GILL-NETTER'S DICTIONARY:
A FRONT ROW SEAT: setting your net right on the district boundary just as the fish are coming in with the tide.
BACKLASH: when a net snags and rips as it comes off the reel.
GETTING LACED OR CORKED: having another fisherman set his net too close to yours.
GETTING TRASHED OR KELPED UP: getting a net full of kelp or driftwood.
HITS: fish visibly hitting and becoming gilled in the net.
SOAKER: keeping one's net in the water for several hours or more.

Traveler's Guide to Fish

COHO SALMON. Size: to 15 pounds. Range: northern California to Bering Sea. Distinguishing features: Adults gunmetal to silver colored, may have small dark flecks or spots on sides. History: Also known as silvers, these are the salmon most frequently caught by sport fishermen. After declining due to foreign fishing in the 1970s and 1980s, silvers made a strong comeback in the 1990s.

CHUM SALMON. Size: 8 to 12 pounds. Range: Oregon to Bering Sea. Distinguishing features: Look remarkably similar to red salmon when *bright*, or freshly returned from ocean. Develop dramatic hooked jaw and mottled colors as spawning approaches. History: Also known as dog salmon from native use as dog food (dried).

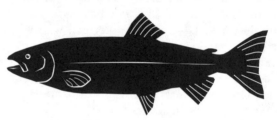

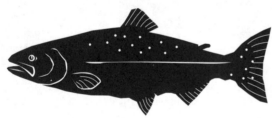

KING SALMON. Size: 15 to 30 pounds; occasionally to more than 100 pounds. Range: northern California to Bering Sea. Distinguishing features: Largest but least abundant salmon; dark spots on tail. History: Also known as chinook or spring salmon, these are prized by smokers for their bright red flesh and high oil content. Construction of Columbia River dams in 1930s and 1940s substantially depleted this species.

PINK SALMON. Size: 2 to 4 pounds. Range: Puget Sound to Bering Sea. Distinguishing features: Smallest and most abundant salmon. Pale pink flesh and small spots on tail, noticeable hump at spawning. Also called humpies.

History: These fish are the target of the purse seine fishery, and primarily processed for canning. Resource is very strong, especially in southeastern Alaska.

SOCKEYE, OR RED SALMON.
Size: 5 to 8 pounds. Range:
Columbia River to Bering Sea.
Distinguishing features: Bright
red flesh, and a faint greenish -
blue tinge on body. History:
Called bluebacks in Canada, and
nicknamed "moneyfish" by American seiners, this is the most commercially valuable species. Spends a year in a freshwater lake before going to sea.

HALIBUT. Size: Typically 50 to
100 pounds; can reach 500
pounds. Range: California to
Bering Sea. Distinguishing features: Flounderlike, but very
much larger. Two eyes on dark
brown top side, underside
white. History: Fished heavily since 1890s, when first iced railway shipments to
East Coast began. After over-fishing, resource was managed back to abundance by
joint U.S. - Canadian International Pacific Halibut Commission.

RED SNAPPER (RED ROCKFISH). Size:
5 to 10 pounds; occasionally to 20
pounds. Range: California to Bering Sea.
Distinguishing features: Dramatic red
color and sharp spines on forward dorsal
fin. History: Because of low abundance,
these are not a major commercial
species. Mostly caught incidentally by
groundfish trawlers and salmon trollers.

LING COD. Size: to 5 feet and 60
pounds plus. Range: California to
Bering Sea. Distinguishing marks:
mottled sides, dark black to blue-
green, lighter on bottom. History
: Common all along northeastern
shore of Pacific, taken commer-
cially by trawl and longline. Sports fishermen usually jig for this species. Flesh is
white, except sometimes in smaller fish, where it is green.

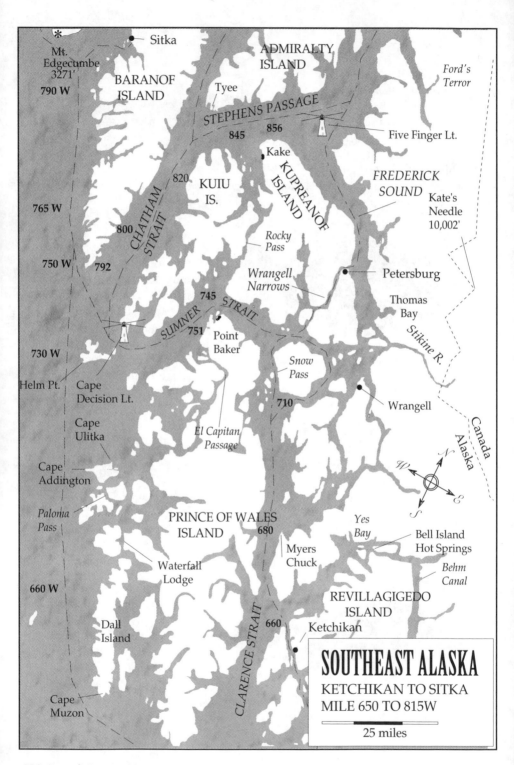

Sitka

ADMIRALTY ISLAND

Mt. Edgecumbe 3271'

790 W

BARANOF ISLAND

Tyee

STEPHENS PASSAGE

Ford's Terror

845   **856**

Five Finger Lt.

Kake

KUPREANOF ISLAND

FREDERICK SOUND

Kate's Needle 10,002'

820

KUIU IS.

765 W

CHATHAM STRAIT

800

Rocky Pass

750 W   **792**

Wrangell Narrows

Petersburg

Thomas Bay

745

STRAIT

Stikine R.

SUMNER

751

Point Baker

Snow Pass

730 W

Helm Pt.

Cape Decision Lt.

710

Wrangell

Canada Alaska

Cape Ulitka

El Capitan Passage

Cape Addington

N
W ⊕ *E*
S

Paloma Pass

PRINCE OF WALES ISLAND

680

Yes Bay

Bell Island Hot Springs

660 W

Myers Chuck

Behm Canal

Waterfall Lodge

REVILLAGIGEDO ISLAND

Dall Island

CLARENCE STRAIT

660

Ketchikan

Cape Muzon

SOUTHEAST ALASKA
KETCHIKAN TO SITKA
MILE 650 TO 815W

25 miles

CHAPTER 5

Islands Without Number

KETCHIKAN, MILE 650, TO JUNEAU, MILE 930

There are forbidden words that no one may utter, either on deck or in fo'c's'le: horse, pig, or hog. They are taboo. According to an old and well established superstition, the mere mention of one of those animals is enough to bring bad weather, poor fishing, snarls on your gear, a line in the propeller, or any other trouble you care to mention. It is deemed very bad manners, if nothing worse, to mention these unmentionable words.
—A.K. Larssen and Sig Jaeger, The ABCs of Fo'c's'le Living.

THE SEA IN THEIR BLOOD. In few places in the United States is the sea so intertwined with the lives of residents as it is here. From the Pennock Island resident (it's directly across from Ketchikan) who goes across Tongass Narrows in his outboard boat for groceries to the black cod fisherman who knows the bottom of Chatham Strait better than his backyard, the waterways of this New England-size maze of islands are part of southeastern Alaska life.

Look for brooms tied in the upper rigging of purse seine salmon vessels. A sign of very good fishing, a broom means a vessel has caught at least 100,000 fish. When prices were good in the late 1980s—50 cents a pound for pink salmon—that translated to $200,000 or more, but when the price plummeted a few years later to 10 or 15 cents, a one-broom season meant barely breaking even.

Ketchikan is known as the Salmon Capital of the World, from the 1930s and '40s when 11 canneries operated here and in nearby inlets. Today, two big canneries and several small freezer plants operate in town, but the resource is strong again after a prolonged slump in the 1970s. You may have heard that salmon are scarce, even in danger of extinction, in northwest states. Actually, the greatest threat to the Alaskan fishing industry in recent years has been competition from farmed Atlantic salmon.

On a weekend, perhaps a hundred of the graceful 58-foot "limit seiners" (Alaska limits the length of salmon seiners to 58 feet) might be tied up along the wharves of Ketchikan, the young crews "uptown" for whatever entertainment they might find. On Sunday they'll leave, dispersed to hundreds of

Fish Traps and Crick Robbers

If there was one burr under Alaskans' saddles, spurring the push for statehood (1959), it was the fish traps. Made of netting and hung from big, floating log frames or from piles driven in shallow water, the traps caught migrating salmon and held them alive until a trap tender could take them to a cannery. Alaskans resented that most of the traps were owned by Seattle companies and the fisheries were managed by the federal government.

Each trap had a watchman. Trap robbers or fish pirates would approach the trap at night and threaten or, more

Brailing a fish trap, circa 1940. Such devices, mostly owned by Seattle fishing companies, were banned shortly after Alaska became a state in 1959.

commonly, pay off the watchman and make off with whatever fish they could load. Few Alaskans frowned on this, feeling that the Seattle-owned canneries were stealing their resource to start with. It depended on the watchman, though.

"The cannery told me it wasn't worth getting shot over a few fish, so if pirates came, I was to let them have what they wanted. But I decided no pirate was taking fish when I was watching, so the first one that came, sneaking around in a big boat with no lights on one night, I got my rifle and shot out his pilothouse windows, and I didn't have no trouble after that." —A fish trap watchman.

"Crick robbing" is the practice of fishing in closed areas, typically the mouths of creeks or rivers where spawning fish congregate. Today, to deter such robbing, "fish cops" patrol in floatplanes, and college students are hired to camp on the creeks and count fish.

coves and bays for the week's fishing.

Look east for the big pulp mill in Wards Cove at **mile 654**. This is the Ketchikan Pulp Company, the engine that has driven the local and regional economy since it was built in 1954. Trees cut throughout lower southeastern Alaska were towed here to become "dissolving pulp," a product used in the manufacture of cellulose-based products such as rayon and cellophane. Today, because of a diminished market and reduced availability of timber, the mill operates at partial capacity.

The deeply indented land to the west at Guard Islands, **mile 660**, is Prince of Wales Island, the third largest island in the United States. From these shores and others like it come the fish and the logs that are the mainstays of the region's economy.

Joe Upton

Salmon purse seiner in Chatham Strait. Generations of young men have put themselves through college by working on these graceful vessels.

The wide channel to the northeast at Guard Islands is Behm Canal, which narrows to less than a half-mile at Behm Narrows and continues east and south, putting Ketchikan on an island.

Sixteen miles up the canal is Traitors Cove, where Vancouver had his closest brush with death. Low on food, circumnavigating Revillagigedo Island in the launch and the yawl boat, his party was nearly overwhelmed by the natives before the other boat could get close enough to aid them. He attributed their behavior to bitter trading experiences with other Europeans, the natives exchanging the best they had for goods that turned out to be shoddily made of inferior materials.

Twelve miles farther north is Yes Bay, where a hand logger in 1925 almost knocked an airplane out of the sky with a tree. The huge cliff-top spruce W.H. Jackson had just cut was toppling toward the water far below when he heard a motor. Horrified, he spotted a Fish and Wildlife floatplane almost directly beneath him, flying low along the beach looking for fish pirates. It was a close call.

Close call with Tlingit natives

A particularly mean deadhead, in a Sumner Strait tide rip. Such dangerous logs, perhaps 70 feet long and weighing several tons, are the scourge of mariners in these waters.

Joe Upton

Of course, bears like salmon streams too. A pilot dropping a young man and his gear at a fish-counting station inquired if he'd brought a gun for the bears.

"Bears?" the young man answered shakily, "No one said anything about bears."

"Here," said the pilot, handing him a small pistol, "take this. It's only a .38—it won't stop a brownie—but you can shoot yourself with it if you get cornered."

North from Ketchikan the Inside Passage goes up Clarence Strait, where Vancouver checked every significant side channel to make sure none was the strait he sought. When the wind blows, especially in the fall, this can be a difficult stretch of water for small craft.

Beach Logging

The shores throughout the region are littered with logs that have broken loose from log rafts. In recent years, the rising price of timber has spawned a practice known as beach logging. A man with a boat and the time, after bidding on and securing the rights to a specific stretch of shore from the U.S. Forest Service, will spend the winter hauling logs off the beaches, assembling them into rafts and towing them to the mill.

Sometimes the loggers are families who camp on the beach in winter to get their rafts together. They get paid when the raft arrives at the mill. "We worked all winter to get them logs, tenting on the beach and going to town once a month for grub. We had a year's paycheck there, had some land all picked out to buy. Then it come up from the south, halfway across Clarence Strait, when the tug was towing the raft to the mill. Broke up the raft and scattered them logs along a hundred miles of shore. Never got a penny out of it, all gone, just like that." —An Alaskan beach logger.

Joe Upton

"October 26, 1974, Ratz Harbor, Clarence Strait, Alaska. Third day blown into this narrow gut of a bay, waiting for weather good enough to travel. This morning squally, but the wind eased by noon, so set off to the south. Got only eight miles before being turned around by violent squall and rips. Lucky to make it back to the harbor to lick our wounds without getting a window busted out by the seas. Grub locker so low had to trade booze to beach loggers for frozen pork chops and instant spuds."

Floating home on Clarence Strait. With little land available for purchase, enterprising Alaskans sometimes built their homes on rafts of logs and moored them in protected coves.

LAND: So how come there's no one living along that great waterfront? The irony of Southeast, and indeed most of Alaska, is there is so little land to buy. The reason is most of it belongs to the federal government and is protected in some way — national forests, national monuments and the like. Entrepreneurs who wished to use the bays of the region as sites for sports fishing lodges, but were unable to buy the land, have built floating lodges which they moor in sheltered bays. They fly in the customers by floatplane.

A few residents have also built floating homes: houses on log rafts, moored between tiny islands or in sheltered nooks in remote bays.

Thorne Bay, west of **mile 680**, is the largest logging camp in Alaska and the source of most of the logs that feed the Ketchikan mills. The camp is hidden from sight, but you may see tugs coming out of the bay with log rafts bound for the mill at Wards Cove.

Look for hand-trollers in the vicinity of Myers Chuck.

Myers Chuck, hidden in a crack in the eastern shore at about **mile 686**, is one of a handful of roadless fishing communities scattered throughout the region. In the late 1930s, the crew of the Maggie Murphy stopped here, still looking for the fishing bonanza for which they had come so far.

"We found a feud raging in the harbor that was as ancient and fierce as that waged between picnickers and ants. The most tedious chore the cabin dweller knows is keeping up a supply of firewood. In Alaska, stoves burn continuously for nine months of the year, and they consume prodigious amounts of fuel. All this fuel must be obtained by felling trees and chopping them into cordwood.

"Where fishermen are living on boats, the problem is even more acute. While most boats have oil stoves, many still have old fashioned wood burners, and the owners must make frequent trips ashore in search of fuel. In Myers Chuck, the fishermen who lived in boats piled their stove wood on the float alongside the point where they habitually docked at night.

"Once Ed and I watched a fisherman creep out of his boat and approach a nearby woodpile. He gazed furtively about to see if anyone was watching, then lifted the canvas, deftly grabbed a slab of wood, and dashed back to his boat. A few minutes later we heard him chopping, and it wasn't long before clouds of smoke were billowing from his stove pipe.

"When the owner of the firewood came to dock, he took inventory of his woodpile and promptly missed one piece.

"Gathering firewood is the god-awfulest job in this country!" he roared, "A man that'll steal it ought to be strung up like a cattle rustler."

—John Joseph Ryan, *The Maggie Murphy*.

The chuck has a really narrow entrance, perhaps 30

Message in a Bottle

Found in a bottle near Port Alexander, Chatham Strait, July 1975:

"Dear Finder:
I, Barnaby Ellis, age ten, live in West Vancouver, B.C. My address is 3024 Proctor Ave. I threw this bottle from the M/V Klondike on our journey to Alaska, May 25, 1975."

Joe Upton

yards wide. Before radar, the mail and freight boat operators would pick their way into the harbor in thick or snowy weather by tooting their horn and listening for the echoes off the steep rocks on either side of the entrance.

Beaver taking off. These husky radial-engined aircraft are especially popular with southeastern Alaska pilots.

Larger ships turn northeast into Stikine Strait at mile 710. Smaller vessels shortcut through Snow Passage at mile 720.

Look for humpback whales feeding in this area. These 40- to 50-foot mammals seem especially to like the tide rips in Snow Passage.

If you're really fortunate and have strong binoculars, you may be able to observe bubble net feeding, a method used by humpback whales to herd fish such as herring into compact, easy-to-eat schools. The whale circles beneath the herring, exhaling slowly from its blow hole. The circle of bubbles serves to contain or herd the fish, and the humpback then surfaces in the middle of the school with its mouth open.

Whale stories: Do orcas (killer whales) take revenge? In British Columbia they tell the story of a logger who, sighting an orca below him as he was falling a tree, dropped it on the whale for sport. Onlookers said the whale appeared to be hurt but swam away. Later that day, the logger got in an outboard to motor across the inlet. Halfway across, a killer whale struck and capsized the boat, and the logger drowned.

Inuit Eskimos on Alaska's North Slope tell a similar tale. A whaler harpooned an orca instead of his usual quarry, the much larger bowhead. After that, whenever he would go down to his skin boat, orcas would be waiting for him, and he was afraid to go out. He finally had to give up fishing and whaling altogether.

Look for Wrangell east of mile 728E.

Look for the village of Wrangell, seven miles east of mile 728E. The muddy water sometimes seen near here is from the Stikine River, six miles north of town. Before 1900, eager hordes from three different gold rushes ebbed and flowed through this town to board steamboats headed up-river. The Stikine Strike occurred in 1861, followed by the Cassiar Strike in 1873, and the Yukon Strike in 1897; for a while Wrangell was the busiest spot in the new Alaska territory. But when John Muir arrived by steamer from Portland in 1879, the town was between rushes. The human tide had ebbed; it was life in the slow lane.

"The most inhospitable place at first sight I had ever seen. The little steamer that had been my home in the wonderful trip through the archipelago, after taking the mail, departed on her return to Portland, and as I watched her gliding out of sight in the dismal blurring rain, I felt strange-

John Muir in Alaska

The naturalist came to Alaska at a limbo period in the place's history. He arrived in 1879, just 12 years after the territory was purchased from Russia, but 18 years before the gold strike that kicked off its modern history.

Few have come as prepared. With a powerful writing style that reflected a boy-hood spent memorizing Bible verses in Scotland and decades of hiking the California Sierra Nevada behind him, he was the preeminent naturalist of his time.

Muir had neither Thinsulate nor Gore-Tex, no North Face tents, Kevlar canoes or Coleman camp stoves. Yet in his five trips to Alaska, he made journey after journey that most of today's outdoors people wouldn't attempt. And he wrote—glorious prose, some of the best ever written about Alaska.

"Of all the thousands of camp-fires I have elsewhere built none was just like this one, rejoicing in triumphant strength and beauty in the heart of the rain laden gale. It was wonderful—the illumined rain and clouds mingled together and the trees glowing against the jet background, the colors of the mossy, lich-ened trunks with sparkling streams pouring down the furrowed bark, and the grey bearded old patriarchs bowing low and chanting in passionate worship."

— John Muir, *Travels in Alaska*.

Joe Upton

Child and dog aboard fish-buying vessel Rosalie, 1972.

ly lonesome.... There was nothing like a tavern or lodging-house in the village, nor could I find any place in the stumpy, rocky, boggy, ground about it that looked dry enough to camp on until I could find a way into the wilderness to begin my studies."

— John Muir, *Travels in Alaska.*

WRANGELL: Visited by fewer cruise ships, Wrangell has a slower pace. Visitors can expect to be greeted by children selling garnets (a dark-purple stone) gleaned from a ledge in the Stikine River, five miles north of town. A half-mile walk south of the dock in Wrangell Harbor is Shakes Island, with impressive totems and an exquisite replica of a Tlingit lodge.

If the tide is down, consider a mile walk to the petroglyphs, which are native carvings on the rocks. Walk along the water for a mile north of the cruise ship dock to the big rock at the end of the beach.

Want to see the country? Charter boats offer tours of the Stikine River flats and dramatic, iceberg-filled Le Conte Bay. Another option would be a boat trip to the Anan Creek bear observatory, 30 miles south, where you'll see bears feeding on spawning salmon. Short on time? Consider a floatplane or helicopter trip. Ask the pilot to take a swing over Petersburg and down Wrangell Narrows.

Look for the entrance to Wrangell Narrows, due north at **mile 741E**. All Vancouver found was a muddy slough in September of 1793; but industrious fishermen and loggers, aided by the Coast Guard and Corps of Engineers' dredges, have dug out the thin spots and put in 65 buoys and markers. They created a 20-mile shortcut between Sumner Strait and Frederick Sound. Most cruise ships are too long and deep to go through here, which is too bad. The scenery is dramatic, like a river through the woods, and the route knocks 90 miles off the run to Juneau.

The Alaska state ferries and small cruise ships, however, do take this route, generally going through when the tide is high, although sometimes at night and sometimes in fog. In such conditions, their skippers are doubly challenged, as not only does the tidal current run hard, but in places it runs obliquely across the dredged channel.

If your ship goes through Wrangell Narrows, even if it's the middle of the night—get up, it's worth it! Consider this foggy meeting between a big ferry and a 70-foot fish packer.

> "I hate to go through them narrows in the black and the fog, but the cannery wanted the fish, so we had to go. Then right in the narrowest place, the radio blasts in my ear: 'This

The tides split in Wrangell Narrows (i.e., flood from north and south). Check your tide book.

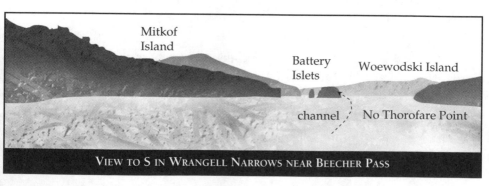

Mitkof Island

Battery Islets

Woewodski Island

channel

No Thorofare Point

VIEW TO S IN WRANGELL NARROWS NEAR BEECHER PASS

Joe Upton

The sea provides. A Point Baker troller picks his herring net.

is the Alaska ferry Matanuska, southbound at marker 16. Northbound traffic please advise.' The Matanuska? Just a mile ahead, and him with the tide pushing him on? I called him right back, and mister, I could hear the tension in that man's voice. 'Matanuska back. Yeah... I see you on my radar... but you'd better pull over and let us by... it's pretty damn tight here.' We were right below Burnt Island Reef, and I could see his target on the radar getting bigger and bigger all the time, and I knew it was time to get the hell out of the way. So I just slowed down and pulled over into the shallows. I'd rather put 'er ashore on a mud bank than get T-boned by a 400-foot ferry!

"I slowed right down until I was just idling into the current, and looked out into the black, trying to see him. You know how it is with that radar: when something gets really close, it just disappears into the sea clutter in the middle of the screen and you can't really tell exactly where it is. Well, the ferry did that, he was that close. I was just bracing myself to hit either the shore or him, when I saw him—just a glimpse of a row of portholes rushing by fast in the night, the big tide pushing him on, and then he was gone. Man, I don't know how them fellows do it, but I know I wouldn't have liked to been him that night."

—An Alaskan tender skipper.

Look for the Sumner Strait salmon gill-net fleet from **mile 740** to about **mile 743**, typically fishing from Sunday noon to Thursday noon. The fish come from the west here, and the trick is to set your net back from the district boundary at Point Baker, so that the ebbing current carries you to the line, then stops, just as the tide turns. This gives you a front row seat, with no room for another boat to set legally

Point Baker is a center for hand-trolling

between you and the incoming fish.

It was this strongly flowing tidal current that caused Captain Johnny O'Brien's luck to run out in the black of a November night in 1917. The *Mariposa* was one of the finest steamers on the Alaska run, but while Dynamite Johnny caught a nap in his stateroom as a pilot steered, the strong current set her off course and onto Mariposa Reef, **mile 745**, where parts of her still remain.

Watch for humpback whales at Point Baker, usually in close to the shore, west of the point. Typically a pair remains here for most of the summer, feeding on herring in the tide rips. In the 1960s, a particular whale got to be known as Ma Baker. Local lore has it that she once surfaced under one of the puddle jumpers, or small fishing skiffs, lifting the surprised fisherman and his boat completely clear of the water for a moment.

This bay was the occasion of one of Vancouver's close calls. Late on the afternoon of September 8, 1793, while exploring and charting Sumner Strait, the party sought shelter before an approaching storm.

"We had scarcely furled the sails, when the wind shifting to the S.E., the threatened storm from that quarter began to blow, and continued with increasing violence during the whole night; we had, however, very providentially reached

Petersburg

On the eastern shore of Wrangell Narrows at its junction with Frederick Sound is Petersburg, a tidy town whose primarily Norwegian-descent residents concentrate on fishing. Petersburg fishermen have a reputation all over the state for their stamina and skill at catching fish. Before the advent of mechanical refrigeration, Petersburg halibut were packed in ice from Le Conte Glacier, shipped by steamer to Seattle, and then by rail to the East Coast.

The Norwegian heritage of the town is visible in the gaily decorated houses and storefronts and celebrated at the Little Norway Festival in mid-May.

The tide running swiftly past the docks and fish processing plants poses a particular challenge to the heavily loaded vessels who must make a landing at the wharves.

Walk north on Front Street past the big cannery, where a view may be had of the narrows and its dramatic current. At times, pickup truck-size pieces of ice make their way into the narrows from Le Conte Glacier.

Joe Upton

My neighbor Flea, a hand-troller, Point Baker, 1973.

an anchorage that completely sheltered us from its fury, and most probably from imminent danger, if not from total destruction. Grateful for such an asylum, I named it Port Protection."
          —Captain George Vancouver, *A Voyage of Discovery*.

It was at last light that Lieutenant Broughton in the Chatham had seen the entrance to what looked like a cove and signalled Vancouver to follow him into the bay, south of mile 745.

Looking north from Port Protection, the land seems to knit together at the head of the distant bay. To the west is Kuiu Island; to the east, Kupreanof Island. Between them is Keku Strait, known locally as Rocky Pass, a popular shortcut for small craft before the Coast Guard removed the navigational markers in the late 1970s as not cost-effective.

Though the markers are gone, Rocky Pass is still used.

Near Rocky Pass in August, 1794, Lieutenant Johnstone, exploring in Vancouver's small boats, was approached by several canoes, with natives who apparently wanted to trade.

"One of the canoes now advanced before the rest, in which a chief stood in the middle of it, plucking the white feathers from the rump of an eagle and blowing them into the air, accompanied by songs and other expressions, which were received as tokens of peace and friendship."
          —Captain George Vancouver.

Helm Point is the most dramatic headland in Southeast Alaska.

However, ever since the near-disastrous struggle with natives at Traitors Cove the previous summer, Vancouver's men were wary of situations in which they were outnumbered. So they declined the invitation to stop and went on to Point Macartney, where they anchored and slept in the boats after 24 hours at the oars.

Hole in the Wall, east of **mile 751**, is one of southeastern Alaska's special places. A channel, so narrow trollers must use care if their poles are down, leads to a tranquil and lakelike basin where deer and bear may be seen along the shore.

At **mile 773**, an hour or so past Point Baker, the vessel track turns sharply northward again at Cape Decision Light and into Chatham Strait.

Look for dramatic Helm Point, a conspicuous headland on Coronation Island, 10 miles south. Rising sheer from the sea to a thousand feet, ending abruptly in a flat, bluff-like tableland, it is the nesting place for thousands of sea birds.

The bays of Coronation Island have a bad reputation among fishermen for williwaws: violent, unpredictable gusts of wind.

"Fishermen are not certain what causes the williwaws. They only know that on peaceful summer evenings, when the sea is calm and boats are resting at anchor, a dull roaring noise is sometimes heard in the harbors of Coronation Island. The noise gains steadily in volume, and suddenly, with terrifying force and swiftness, a blast of wind sweeps down off the rocky hills, scattering boats like bowling pins."

—John Joseph Ryan, *The Maggie Murphy.*

In calm waters, vessels may tie together for more convivial traveling.

Joe Upton

UWSC Thwaites 0098-1

Getting in the winter's meat, Southeast Alaska style.

Sitka, Via Cape Ommaney and Outside

Sitka-bound vessels join the outside track at the steep promontory of Cape Ommaney at **mile 750W**. Look for trollers fishing nearby. You may see some of the very small hand-trolling skiffs based out of Port Alexander fishing in the ocean swells here.

Study the shoreline carefully north of the cape: it is distinctly different from inside waters, where the vegetation frequently grows down to the water's edge. Outside shores show the effect of winter storms, which have washed away the soil in places and exposed bare rock a hundred feet up.

Look for the buoys and flags of longline gear, especially between Cape Ommaney and Cape Decision, where your course line crosses the edges of the deep underwater canyon popular with halibut and black cod fishermen. Sitka is the center for a substantial fleet of longline vessels which sometimes work this vicinity.

These waters are popular with longliners.

While almost every bay in Chatham Strait, 30 miles east of here, had a fish plant of sorts during the last century, the bays along the outside are conspicuously without cannery ruins, primarily because of their more remote location and more exposed nature.

Look for the high, thin waterfall in Byron Bay, visible from **mile 764W**.

Small craft take a shortcut to Sitka through the islands east of mile 794W. The Mount Fuji-shaped volcano, visible depending on conditions from **mile 790W** northward, is 3,271-foot Mount Edgecumbe, the landfall for mariners coming across the North Pacific Ocean.

To Juneau via Inside

For much of this century, Chatham Strait was a beehive of activity. Between the salmon plants, the herring plants, and the whaling stations, almost every bay in this canyonlike region was home to some sort of commercial activity. Then the herring and the whales disappeared, and refrigerated tenders allowed consolidation of the salmon canneries into towns like Petersburg and Ketchikan.

For many of the plant operators, who were headquartered in Seattle, the decision to close a plant came in the wintertime, when just a caretaker remained in the remote Chatham Strait bay. Sometimes it was easier to abandon the plant than to send up a vessel and a crew to bring out the supplies. The plants were in reality whole little towns, with well-built houses for the managers and their families, bunkhouses and mess halls, warehouses, workshops, powerhouses, and so forth. When they were no longer needed, the owners just walked away, leaving the warehouses full of supplies. Word that the company in a particular

A Hand-troller's Life

"Port Alexander, June 1975:

"Visited Amy and Scott in their little cabin on the upper lagoon today. With a garden in back and his beautiful 14-foot hand-trolling skiff in front, they've come a long ways since the last time I heard about them.

"That was last year, and she was very pregnant. They were squatting at a tumbledown cannery in Pillar Bay and trying to make a living handtrolling from his small open boat. The fishing was poor, so they moved south to Port Malmesbury and camped on the beach. There was a fish buyer there, but when he needed medicine or groceries the fish buyer didn't have, he'd take that little skiff of his all the way across Chatham Strait to Port Alexan-

Scott's skiff

der. Those are big waters for an open boat, and he told me once that old engine pounding away was the only thing between him and a pretty cold and wild sea.

"Now, with a fat baby nursing, a garden planted, a pile of firewood outside, good fishing here, and friends all around, it looks as if he's about got 'er licked."

MOHAI

Sperm whale, Port Armstrong, circa 1940. Today protected by law, several species of whales frequent Alaskan waters.

bay had "jerked their watchman" was notice that it was free pickings, and the region's fishermen and trappers were quick to make sure nothing was wasted.

For the small craft traveler, it is almost spooky to travel in lower Chatham Strait, to anchor and go ashore and wander through the ruins, rarely encountering another traveler.

> "June 4, 1972, Chatham Strait. The day came cloudless and still. We pulled the anchor in the pale predawn off another lifeless cannery, slipped out into the empty strait, and put the gear in the water before the sun came over the mountains. Just us and one other boat in maybe a hundred miles of shoreline."

Hidden in a fold on the flank of Baranof Island, west of **mile 792**, is Port Alexander. With a good harbor, a settlement, a fish buyer and a store, and good fishing at Cape Ommaney (west of **mile 786**), it's a popular spot in summer. In its heyday, the 1920s and 1930s, it was Alaska with a capital A, as the Maggie Murphy boys noted.

> "It became the number one trolling port in the territory, a wide open, carefree, money-kissed little place that old-timers still recall with nostalgia."
> —John Joseph Ryan, *The Maggie Murphy*.

When they walked into town, they were halted by an elderly man who told them, "Boys, it's illegal to walk on the streets of Port Alexander sober."

In those days, many trollers worked out of open boats, some without motors, rowing as they towed their lines through the water. A little tent city sprang up south of the dock each summer. By the late 1940s the party was over, the great runs rapidly diminishing as the newly built dams on the Columbia River, 1,200 miles south, prevented the big kings from reaching their spawning grounds.

Port Conclusion, three miles north of Port Alexander, was where Vancouver anxiously awaited the four overdue cutters and yawl boats that were filling in the last blank places on his chart. On the afternoon of the 19th of August, 1794, the boats hove safely into sight during a rainstorm.

With grog for all hands, and cheers ringing from ship to ship in a remote cove halfway around the world from England, there ended one of the most remarkable feats of navigation and exploration in modern times. In three summers of exploring and charting this unknown coast, through persistent fogs, swift currents, occasional thick ice, losing just one man to bad shellfish, Vancouver had disproved the ages-old notion of the Northwest Passage. In doing so, he charted, explored, described and named much of the Northwest coast. It was nothing less than a stunning achievement. He was 38 years old.

To the west at **mile 800** is Port Walter, the wettest place on the United States mainland, with 240 inches of rain a year.

Unusual Places

Kootznahoo Inlet, north of the Tlingit village of Angoon on the western side of Admiralty Island, is a narrow channel leading tortuously east to 10,000 acres of intricate channels, lagoons and bays.

On a large tide, the current boils in through the entrance, swirling at up to 10 knots. Some of the passages to the inner waters appear more like

Humpback whale blowing in the contricted waters of Kootznahoo Inlet.

creeks in the forest, through which the water seems to tumble downhill into the basins and lagoons. At slack water, humpback whales have entered as far as the native village, feeding on herring. Considering their size, the current and the constricted nature of the passage, it seems remarkable that none have stranded.

THS

At the head of the bay is the very dramatic inlet to Big Port Walter, an unusually steep-sided basin containing the village like ruins of a herring plant. A vessel approaching the head of the outer bay might not be aware of the inner basin until the entrance appears as a crack in the canyon wall. Through this crack passed the Standard Oil tanker when the herring plant inside was operating.

One wonders about the spirits of the winter caretaker, with the sun gone over the mountain on October 15, not to appear again for four or five months, and the inner basin frozen eight to ten feet thick.

Bay of Pillars, east of **mile 813**, and Washington Bay, east of **mile 820**, both contained substantial herring or salmon processing plants in their day. In a visit to Washington Bay in 1975, the buildings were intact, but the forest was growing up around them.

Likewise, Tyee, now abandoned, at the southern tip of Admiralty Island, was a major salmon cannery in the 1940s, the brightest lights for miles around.

Look southeast from around **mile 845** to the head of the island-choked bay and to Rocky Pass, the narrow back channel to Sumner Strait. It was this narrow channel ("we paddled on through the midst of the innumerable islands") from which John Muir, an evangelist companion and a group of native paddlers emerged on the morning of October 19, 1879. The natives dreaded the crossing of Frederick Sound to Point Gardner at the southern tip of Admiralty Island.

Four-masted ship Star of Greenland *at Loring Cannery. A fleet of these tall ships carried supplies north and canned salmon south right up until World War II.*

"Toyatte said he had not slept a single night thinking of it, and after we rounded Cape Gardner and the comparatively smooth Chatham Strait, they all rejoiced, laughing and chatting like frolicsome children." — John Muir, Travels in Alaska.

The village visible to the southeast from **mile 845** is Kake, a Tlingit village supported by a cannery and logging on native land. It was here, according to one story, that around 1970 the surprised residents greeted a tug towing a big barge. The tug had come up through Rocky Pass. No one could remember such a vessel or barge coming through the extremely narrow passage before. The skipper of the tug came out of the pilot-house and hailed those on shore.

"Say," the rough-looking man said, waving a hand back toward Rocky Pass, "that Wrangell Narrows ain't nothing like the chart." He stopped and looked over at the village on the shore, "And I thought Petersburg was larger than this." He was 40 miles west of where he thought he was.

Watch for floating ice in Stephens Passage

THE FIRST OF THE ICE: Start looking for ice at Turnabout Island, **mile 856**. This is the southern limit of drift ice from the glaciers in Tracy Arm, east of **mile 900**, and Le Conte Glacier, east of Petersburg. On occasion Le Conte Glacier puts out tremendous amounts of ice, some of which may find its way into Wrangell Narrows.

Five Finger Light, at **mile 870**, was the first manned lighthouse in Alaska and the last one automated, in 1983. Compared to other coastal areas, Alaska has relatively few lighthouses because of the difficulty of building and supplying such structures in remote areas. Wherever possible the Coast Guard relies on buoys and untended lights for navigational aids.

Look for humpback whales throughout Frederick Sound

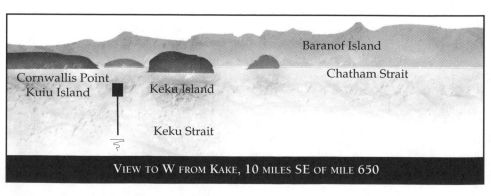

Baranof Island

Chatham Strait

Cornwallis Point
Kuiu Island

Keku Island

Keku Strait

VIEW TO W FROM KAKE, 10 MILES SE OF MILE 650

Joe Upton

Victrola in abandoned fox farm, Harbor Island, east of mile 900.

and Stephens Passage. Much larger than orcas, up to 50 feet long, humpbacks sometimes breach—leap completely clear of the water—a good trick for a 30-ton creature.

Bound to or from Petersburg? Your vessel track swings east at Cape Fanshaw, **mile 866**, and follows Frederick Sound for 35 miles to Wrangell Narrows.

"Around noon we rounded Cape Fanshaw, scudding swiftly before a fine breeze, to the delight of our Indians, who had now only to steer and chat. Here we overtook two Hoona Indians and their families on their way home from Fort Wrangell. They had exchanged five sea otter skins, worth about a hundred dollars apiece, and a considerable number of fur-seal, land-otter, martin, beaver, and other furs and skins, $800 worth, for a new canoe valued at 80 dollars, some flour, tobacco, blankets, and a few barrels of molasses for the manufacture of whiskey. The blankets were not to wear, but to keep

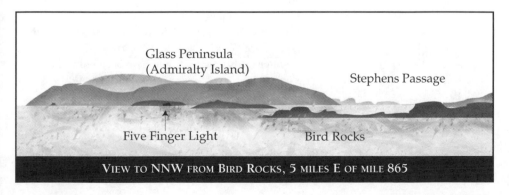

Glass Peninsula
(Admiralty Island)

Stephens Passage

Five Finger Light

Bird Rocks

VIEW TO NNW FROM BIRD ROCKS, 5 MILES E OF MILE 865

as money, for the almighty dollar of these tribes is a Hudson's Bay Blanket."

—John Muir, *Travels in Alaska.*

A little later the two canoes began to race each other, continuing until after dark. The water was "firing" that night: exhibiting phosphorescence, showing each stroke of oar or paddle and the wakes of the canoes as shining tracks in the black. The group was heading for a well-known salmon stream to camp for the night. As they approached, they could see the schools of fish glowing in the water. Muir and his traveling companion set up their tent against the steady rain. The Hoona natives, two families, simply took their rest on the wet ground: "Our Hoona neighbors were asleep in the morning at sunrise, lying in a row, wet and limp like dead salmon."

On the shore of Harbor Island, which guards the entrance to Tracy Arm, west of **mile 900**, is an abandoned homestead and, in the woods behind, empty fox cages of chicken wire, almost completely taken over by the underbrush. Fox farms were common on small southeastern Alaska

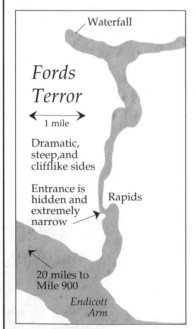

Fords Terror

Waterfall

← 1 mile →

Dramatic, steep, and clifflike sides

Entrance is hidden and extremely narrow

Rapids

← 20 miles to Mile 900

Endicott Arm

Muir discovers Fords Terror by accident.

It was John Muir, exploring in the canoe with his native paddlers, who by accident discovered the dramatic inlet known as Fords Terror, 17 miles southeast of Harbor Island. "When we were tracing this curve, however, in a leisurely way, in search of a good landing, we were startled by Captain Tyeen shouting, 'Skookum chuck! Skookum chuck!' (Strong water, strong water), and found our canoe was being swept sideways by a powerful current, the roar of which we had mistaken for a waterfall. We barely escaped being carried over a rocky bar on the boiling flood, which, as we afterwards learned, would have been only a happy shove on our way." —John Muir, *Travels in Alaska.*

Beyond the rapids is a narrow, dramatic canyon, opening up to a remote and little-visited basin, whose beauty Muir likened to Yosemite (for a time it was called Yosemite Inlet). It is one of southeastern Alaska's special places.

Joe Upton

Iceberg in Stephens Passage near Gambier Bay, mile 880.

islands in the 1940s and 1950s. Typically fed salmon in season, the foxes were a problem to feed when the fish weren't running.

"When we were low on fox food, Dad would send my brother and me over to Point Astley, where there were lots of seals and sea lions. We'd shoot those big sea lions, and then we had to cut the carcasses into pieces with a two-man saw to load into the skiff. God, it was a mess."

—A fox farmer.

TRACY ARM: Traveling up Tracy Arm (the entrance is five miles northeast of **mile 900**) is like going back through geologic history. The fjord's dramatic walls lose their vegetation until, close to the glaciers, they become bare shining rock, shaped and ground smooth by the ice. There is no shore to speak of, the mountains plunging vertically into the water, which in many places is more than a thousand feet deep. Seeking a place to spend the night, Muir and his party tied their canoe to a rock and climbed up a hundred feet on hands and knees to a little ledge, dragging their supplies behind them. Once there, they found a campsite rich with berries, enough fallen wood for a huge fire, and they counted 16 waterfalls across and around the arm.

Use extreme care around icebergs.

TIPS FOR MARINERS: Use care here; some of the bergs calving off these glaciers weigh thousands of tons and create waves up to 25 feet high as they fall into the water. Large bergs may roll over or break up without warning, also creating large and unexpected waves.

Muir was genuinely moved by the power and the beauty of the glaciers, and he was able to communicate some of this enthusiasm to his companions. Once, when they had paddled most of an afternoon up Tracy Arm, frustrated with the narrow and ice-choked channel, they turned yet another corner and found what he had come to seek, the glacier itself. While Muir stood in the canoe, sketching the glacier, several huge icebergs calved off, thundering into the water of the narrow fjord. "The ice mountain is well disposed toward you," one of the native paddlers said to Muir, "He is firing his big guns to welcome you."

Look for icebergs calving off glaciers in Tracy Arm.

IF YOUR SHIP GOES INTO TRACY ARM: When it stops or slows near the glaciers, try to find a place at the rail in the forward part of the vessel, away from the noise of the ship, and listen. The roar is from the many waterfalls tumbling into the gorge. If you are lucky you may hear and see the crack and rumble of a big berg as it calves into the salt water. If none happens to calve while you are watching, look at the size of the icebergs; consider that most of an iceberg is under water, and think what a commotion must be made when such a mass of ice breaks off and falls into the water.

Fish packers or tenders sometimes use icebergs for a head start on getting their fish holds down to the required 32 degrees. Their engine-driven refrigeration systems can take up to 24 hours to chill down a hold full of water so they can take fish. If they can pull up to a big iceberg and pump the frigid water around it into the hold, they can save themselves money and time.

The inlet to the east at **mile 914** is Port Snettisham, at the head of which is a dam supplying power to the Juneau area. The sides of the inlet are so steep the power lines had to be strung by helicopter.

The Southeast Alaska mainland here is narrow, with only 14 miles separating the head of Port Snettisham and the Canadian border, at 6,460-foot Mount Brundage.

Beware the Taku winds.

Taku Inlet is the wide channel leading northeast at **mile 929**; it is the mouth of the Taku River. Vancouver's Lieutenant Whidbey and his party faced sleet, rain and thick ice as they traced the continental boundary here in early August, 1794; they went only 13 miles before being stopped by the ice. Today the glaciers have retreated, and the river is open to the Canadian border and beyond.

There is a powerful phenomenon here: the Taku winds, powerful cold northerlies that blow down the gorge with gale force. When the winds blow, those last 10 miles to Juneau can seem long indeed for small craft waiting them out at Taku Harbor, **mile 920**.

Had the settlement of Alaska proceeded at the same time as, say, Boston, or Philadelphia, five thousand miles to the east and south, it is unlikely that anyone would have chosen Juneau for a town site. According to Vancouver, Gastineau Channel was impassable because of the ice, and his men passed through in August.

Hood Bay cannery room number 12 waits for workers who will never return.

Indeed, the conclusion that the climate was substantially colder in the late 1700s than it is today is inescapable. Consider this description of the mountains of the east side of Lynn Canal in August, 1794, "Those lofty frozen mountains...rose abruptly from the water side, and were covered in perpetual snow, while their sides were broken into deep ravines or valleys, filled with immense mountains of ice."

Today the glaciers remain, but they have retreated from the salt water, and only the mountaintops are white in August.

Traveler's Guide to Birds

BALD EAGLE. Size: wingspan to 6 feet and larger. Range: Oregon to Bering Sea. Distinguishing features: Large soaring bird, adult marked with white head and tail, juveniles dark brown or mottled. Notes: Uncommon in Puget Sound, these very noticeable large birds are common throughout coastal British Columbia and Alaska. While scavenging dead fish, they will also attack live fish and small animals.

BONAPARTE'S GULL. Size: to 14 inches. Range: Peru to Bering Sea. Distinguishing marks: smaller than most gulls, easily recognised by black head and bill and white wing tips. Notes: Nests and breeds in interior, migrates south in late summer, returns in spring.

ARCTIC TERN. Size: to 10 inches. Range: Circumpolar. Winters in Antarctica, summers in coastal Alaska and British Columbia. Distinguishing features: Terns are noted for their smaller size, slender shape, and distinctive long forked tail. Arctic terns have a prominent black cap on their heads. Notes: These remarkable birds migrate some 8,000 to 10,000 miles each spring and fall.

COMMON LOON. Size: to 20 inches. Range: California to Bering Sea. Distinguishing features: Large diving bird with sharp bill and noticeable white and black checkerboard pattern on dark back. Notes: Dives when approached. Feeds on fish captured underwater. Requires long flapping takeoff run on windless days. Haunting, whoooo call.

RAVEN. Size: to 24 inches. Range: Central America to Bering Sea. Distinguishing features: Crow-like, but substantially larger. Jet black, almost glossy purple color; call is a distinctive *klok* sound. Notes: The raven is a central figure in Haida and Tlingit mythology; raven figures appear on totem poles and dance masks.

MARBLED MURRELET. Size: 10 inches Range: California to Alaska. Distinguishing marks: Very short neck, marbled white markings on brown. Winter plumage is dark above, white below. Notes: This species, seen commonly in all seasons in Southeast Alaska, may be the next Spotted Owl. Nesting in old growth timber, its numbers are declining.

STELLER'S JAY. Size: to 12 inches. Range: Washington to Bering Sea. Distinguishing features: Bright blue and black coloring with distinctive black crest. Very visible and busy; likes to taunt larger birds, such as eagles. Notes: Named for German naturalist Georg Steller, who was with explorer Vitus Bering, whose 1741 expedition discovered Alaska.

SPOTTED SANDPIPER. Size: to 8 inches. Range: California to Arctic. Distinguishing marks: Easy to identify in summer plumage with large spots underneath. Fall and winter plumage is brown above and white below with no spots. Notes: This little bird is seen over most of the Alaskan coast. When surprised, flies away from the shore with short, jerky wingbeats, and returns nearby.

Juneau

Gastineau Channel was choked with ice when Vancouver's party passed through in August, 1794. Today the ice is gone and the channel forms a sheltered waterway between the Alaska mainland and Douglas Island, through which small craft may pass at high tide.

But the climate is still noticeably colder than that of Ketchikan or Sitka, with an icefield in the mountains just behind town, and Mendenhall Glacier just 12 miles to the north.

1. Douglas Island, once site of Treadwell Mine.
2. River rafting on Mendenhall Lake and River.
3. Gastineau Channel to Auke Bay and Lynn Canal.
4. Mendenhall Glacier and visitor's center.
5. Juneau Douglas Bridge and small craft harbor.
6. Downtown Juneau.
7. "Flightseeing" over glaciers and ice fields.
8. Cruise ship dock and nearby A-J mine ruins.
9. Jet boat wilderness and glacier tours.

7.

6.

8.

9.

Joe Upton

Juneau

For Juneau residents and their many pleasure boats, the wilderness is very close.

"The Glory Hole" was the nickname for the cavernous entrance to the gold mine across Gastineau Channel from Juneau. In those days, at the turn of the century, men were cheap and safety regulations were few. Sometimes a miner a week went to glory—in a cave-in or an accident in the pit and the miles of tunnels that led off it.

Just as it did for the territory, gold put Juneau on the map. But the fine gold in the creeks that Joe Juneau and Richard Harris found in 1880 played out, to be replaced by a very different enterprise: industrial-style hard-rock mining.

The gold at Juneau was embedded in rock, which had to be drilled, blasted, and transported to one of the noisiest contraptions of the industrial age: the stamp mill. This crude device crushed the ore-bearing rock into pieces small enough for chemical removal of the gold to be effective. The Treadwell mill at Juneau was the largest in the world, with 960 stamp machines crushing 5,000 tons of ore a day.

Today the mines are gone; city, state, and federal governments now provide half the jobs in Juneau. The governments are gentler employers.

Cosmopolitan, yet surrounded by wilderness, Juneau is a town where you can come out of an espresso shop and encounter a bear rummaging through a garbage can.

There are many things to do around town; these are some of the editor's choices:

•GO SEE THE ICEFIELDS: In the mountains behind town is the dramatic Juneau Icefield and nearby Mendenhall Glacier. To see the glaciers by air is a remarkable experience, allowing the traveler to comprehend more easily the geology and the dynamics that produce the region's glaciers. If small airplanes are not for you, take the coach tour to Mendenhall Glacier, 14 miles from downtown; the visitors' center at the glacier has a comprehensive display on glaciology.

•RAFT THE MENDENHALL RIVER: Alaska Travel Adventures begin their raft trips on Mendenhall Lake, with great views of the glacier, and follow the Mendenhall River, with a snack of smoked salmon, reindeer sausage, cheese and a beverage along the way. The guides provide rain gear, life jackets and boots. Total trip time, including travel to and from downtown, is three and a half hours.

•FLY-IN TO A SALMON BAKE: The Taku Glacier Lodge, built in 1929 on the Taku River 17 miles northeast of Juneau, offers a unique tour. Floatplanes pick up guests downtown for a dramatic flight over the glaciers and up the Taku River valley to the lodge, where lunch is a fresh-baked king salmon. The three-hour tour (flight included) allows time for exploring the nearby trails.

•WALK AROUND THE TOWN: Like most Southeast Alaska towns, Juneau is small enough to know quickly: just grab a walking-tour map and hit the trail. The neocolonial place with a totem pole out front is the governor's mansion. Don't pass a stop at the Alaska State Museum. And make time for shopping for crafts and gifts around Seward and South Franklin streets.

If you're thinking of including kayaking on your trip, Juneau, with its miles of sheltered waterways, might be a good bet.

Sam and Elsie's Getaway

Thayer Lake Lodge

"Everyone told us we should spend at least some time out in the bush, away from the towns—you know, the real Alaska. Well, somewhere we had read about Thayer Lake Lodge, which they said was 20 minutes by floatplane from Juneau. We made reservations, but nothing prepared us for the tranquility of the place. It was another world, in the way you always think about the wilderness: four small log buildings on this perfect lake, framed by the big woods on all sides. The owners, Edith and Bob Nelson, built it all themselves 40 years ago, and they made us feel like we were part of the family. There were canoes for fishing the lake, we went hiking around the shore, went swimming, but most of all a serenity and peace we had never experienced before. The Nelsons take in just a few guests at a time, the lake is nine miles long—nothing on it but woods—and their power comes from a water wheel, so there's not even generator noise. Sam got in some great fishing, but mostly I just relaxed."

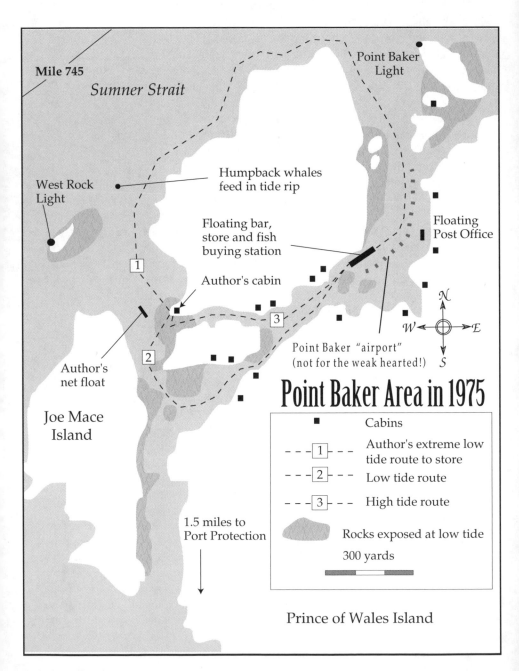

Mile 745

Sumner Strait

Point Baker Light

West Rock Light

Humpback whales feed in tide rip

Floating bar, store and fish buying station

Floating Post Office

Author's cabin

Author's net float

1

2

3

Point Baker "airport" (not for the weak hearted!)

N
W ← → E
S

Joe Mace Island

1.5 miles to Port Protection

Point Baker Area in 1975

■   Cabins

– –1– –   Author's extreme low tide route to store

– –2– –   Low tide route

– –3– –   High tide route

    Rocks exposed at low tide

300 yards

Prince of Wales Island

CHAPTER 6

Life in a Roadless Community

I magine, cheap waterfront land and good fishing close at hand. This was the situation at the remote and roadless communities of Point Baker and nearby Port Protection in the early 1970s (south of **mile 745**). A person could get an acre-sized waterfront lot on a sheltered cove, with the right to harvest 10,000 board feet of timber a year from the adjacent forest for personal use. You could build a cabin out of the trees on your land and make enough cash fishing from an outboard skiff to support a family.

A floating store/bar/fish buyer at Point Baker served the needs of the hundred or so souls settled around these two coves on the edge of the vast woods. The mail and freight boat came once a week, supplemented by the occasional floatplane. Families with gill-netters or trollers tried to make a trip to town — Wrangell or Petersburg, each about 40 miles away, a long day's round trip — every few months to

Puddle jumper near Point Baker, 1974.

Joe Upton

Point Baker from the air: With limited takeoff space and tide rips at the harbor entrance, it was a particular challenge for floatplane pilots.

Strangers should use these narrow channels on a rising tide.

stock up on supplies a little cheaper.

Behind the shore was the forest, thick, almost impenetrable. For the most part walking was so difficult everyone traveled by outboard skiffs or "puddle jumpers." At Point Baker especially, one's traveling decisions were dictated by the tide. Have a whiskey warmup some snowy winter afternoon with your groceries at the store? Stay too late and the trip home might be a nightmare: wading along the shallow channel, towing your skiff behind you, lifting, scraping it over the thin places, picking your way with the flashlight through the snow, and hoping your batteries last until you make it home.

When I arrived here with my wife on our 32-foot gillnetter in the spring of 1972, the flavor of the place was compelling. The older residents welcomed younger blood, and the salmon fishing in Sumner Strait was great. We found part of an island, on a private cove, with a gorgeous western exposure and view, for $17,000, 10 percent down and 10 years to pay.

After the season, in our houseboat on Seattle's Lake Union, we set to making plans for a cabin on our newly purchased land in Point Baker. As our money dwindled, so did the size of our new-home-to-be until whatever roof we could get over our heads for fifteen hundred bucks would have to be it. We settled on a 12-by-16-foot box with a half loft, 250 square feet, total, tiny.

Joe Upton

With tight-fisted determination, we scoured garage sales and discount building suppliers. At a second-hand store we found a big diesel oil range for $35; at another, all our windows and doors for $175. In my tiny floating shop I prefabbed a Formica kitchen counter top, complete with sink and drawers. We got plywood, nails, and shingles, all on deep discount, and purchased a 16-foot cedar skiff with a 10-horsepower 1958 Evinrude outboard. Tool by tool, fitting by fitting, we packed all the supplies and extras aboard my 32-foot gill-net vessel and skiff to tow north.

Retired salmon troller, living aboard boat at Point Baker dock.

The weather gods granted us an easy trip, and shortly after arriving in Point Baker, the mail boat arrived with our pickup truck-sized bundle of lumber from the sawmill in Wrangell, and our first major problem.

The plan was to tow the tightly strapped bundle of lumber through the narrow back channel to our secluded cove and house site. But when the mail boat's crane lowered the bundle of lumber into the water, it kept right on going. The wood was so green and dense it wouldn't float. It was what the locals called "pond dried."

We had to set it temporarily on the dock and then haul it in our skiff, load by load, to our cove.

In the two weeks before the salmon season began we struggled: the wood was so wet it splashed when your ham-

Our front window, 1975.

mer missed the nail. My one and only hand saw bent on the first beam we cut. It rained every day; every night we would take the skiff back to our boat at the Point Baker dock, heat up something quick, and fall, exhausted, shivering, into our sleeping bags.

And we created something exquisite: out every window was the water. As we ate at the driftwood table, we could see eagles swooping low over the cove. There were curious seals, and most marvelous of all, a pair of humpbacks that hung out in the tide rips by West Rock, off the mouth of our cove. On still nights, we could hear the sigh-like breathing of the whales as they surfaced and exchanged fresh air for stale. When the first snow came one November evening, the fire in the wood stove crackled cheerily, our kerosene lamp shone out on the vast and wild world beyond the windows, and it was magic.

Getting in the Firewood, Southeast Alaska Style

At Point Baker on a breezy winter morning, the CB radios crackle from cabin to cabin: good firewood logs have been spotted in the ebbing tide pouring around the tip of the island. Within minutes a handful of skiffs and small fishing craft set out across the mile or so of crooked water between the harbor and the logs. As each arrives, they stop alongside the closest large log, hammer in a big steel staple, attach a tow line, and begin the long, slow tow back to the harbor. The first to arrive latch onto really huge logs, 60 feet long by four feet in diameter, four cords of firewood in a single log. Hauled up on the beach at high tide, such a find would be enough for most of the winter for the smaller cabins.

Joe Upton

Many of the new young people who arrived in the 1970s couldn't afford the price of an outboard and fell back on the traditional puddle jumper, whose origins were in the 1930s and '40s, when so-called hand-trollers (they didn't have engine-operated equipment to haul in the lines) were spread all over Southeast Alaska.

Evening at "Port Upton."

The power plant in the 1970s-vintage Port Protection-to-Point Baker puddle jumper was usually an air-cooled Briggs & Stratton one-cylinder gasoline engine, turning a propeller through a homemade reduction gear of belts and pulleys.

With such a craft, sporting two fresh-cut-from-the-woods trolling poles, a young fisherman or woman could catch perhaps $6,000 to $8,000 worth of fish in the summer, with very little overhead.

A young entrepreneur brought in a portable sawmill and the building boom was on.

THANKSGIVING AT PORT PROTECTION: In the fall of 1973, a good fishing season behind us and excited to be in our new, if small, cabin, we went by outboard to one of the three or four Thanksgiving dinners being held around the cove at Port Protection.

We arrived to a Norman Rockwell scene: the harbor was

Point Baker Scrapbook

Clockwise from upper left: Hand-trolling family; heading for Port Protection through the back channel; view out our kitchen window, Point Baker, Dec. 1973; homesteader, Port

Protection, 1972; building a float with salvaged beach logs and store-bought lumber; wintertime, Port Protection.

still, the daylight was dying, snow was falling, and kerosene lamps burned cheerily in homes along the water's edge.

Tying our skiff to a big moored firewood log, we walked up the beach and went inside a big three-room cabin with attached shop. My wife went in to help the other women, and I stayed in the shop with the men. The wood stove was hot, the rum was flowing and we talked about the hunting and the fishing.

But when we were all called in to sit down, my wife and I learned a new Thanksgiving tradition. It was a big group and a small table, but it wasn't a problem. The men sat down side by side at the table, decorated for the occasion and heaped high with food. The women just sat wherever they could: on the sofas or cross-legged on the floor.

In summer, with daylight that lasted from four in the morning until after eleven at night, the focus was fishing: making enough to make it through the long winter. But when the season was over and the days got shorter, there was time for the kind of relaxed visiting that is a highlight of life in such places.

The center for much of the activity in these two communities was the floating bar and store in the harbor at Point Baker. Built on a raft of logs, one of the most tedious prob-

Heard at the Point Baker Bar

Being a rough-and-tumble sort of place, the Point Baker Bar didn't offer the wide selection of drinks some of the newcomers in town were used to. Once in 1972 two gill-net vessels freshly arrived from Seattle tied up to the bar to celebrate their trip.

Bartender: "What'll it be, fellas?"

Newly arrived fisherman to wife: "What d'ya think, honey, you wanna Manhattan?"

The Point Baker Bar

Joe Upton

Bartender: "Hey guys, we got whiskey and water, whiskey and Coke, and whiskey and Tang. What's it gonna be?"

lems for fishermen drinking in Alaska's harbor towns was avoided: *The Ramp*.

The tides in the region are huge: in a six-hour period the water level might vary 20 feet. Imagine: you come in tired from a fishing trip at high tide, tie up your boat at one of Ketchikan's many marina-style floats, walk across the nearly horizontal ramp to the shore to, say, the Fo'c's'le Bar. There, surrounded by acquaintances, you relive and celebrate many fishing experiences. Six hours later, your vision blurred and equilibrium unsteady, you head back, only to discover that the tide is way down, and the ramp is almost vertical.

Troller's home, Port Protection.

At Point Baker you could tie your boat right up to the bar, with no ramp to negotiate. Not only that, it was less than half a mile from the fishing grounds, and it sold groceries and hardware and bought fish.

Seeking greener pastures, I sold my cabin at Point Baker in the mid 1980's and built a new boat for the remote salmon fishery in Bristol Bay, Alaska, 1,000 miles west. Bleak, austere, remote, with violent tidal currents and few good harbors, it was the opposite of Southeast Alaska. The fishing was a competitive frenzy I'd never experienced before, but there were friends to guide me and the shorter season allowed us more time at home with our families and children.

Yet to a man (Alaska law allows salmon fishermen to only fish a single region), we all missed the wooded waterways and the secluded harbors we'd left behind.

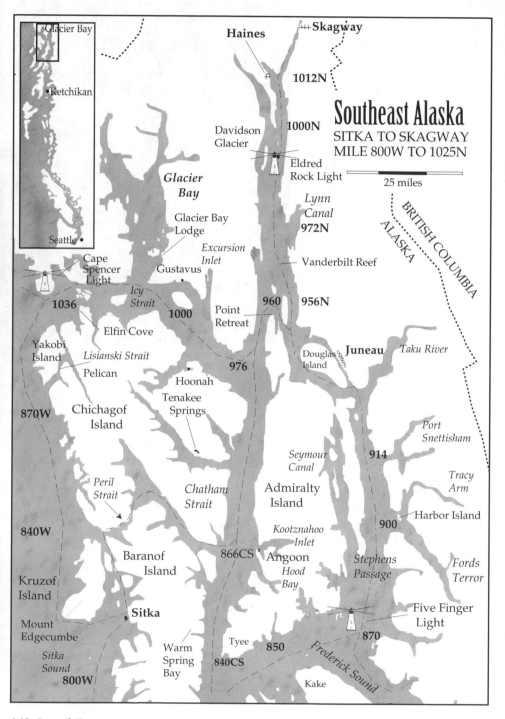

Glacier Bay

Ketchikan

Seattle

Haines

Skagway

1012N

Davidson
Glacier

1000N

Southeast Alaska
SITKA TO SKAGWAY
MILE 800W TO 1025N

Eldred
Rock Light

25 miles

Glacier
Bay

Glacier Bay
Lodge

Lynn
Canal
972N

Excursion
Inlet

Gustavus

Vanderbilt Reef

BRITISH COLUMBIA
ALASKA

Cape
Spencer
Light

Icy
Strait

1036

1000

Point
Retreat

960

956N

Elfin Cove

Yakobi
Island

Lisianski Strait

Pelican

976

Douglas
Island

Juneau

Taku River

Hoonah

870W

Chichagof
Island

Tenakee
Springs

Port
Snettisham

Peril
Strait

Chatham
Strait

Seymour
Canal

914

Tracy
Arm

840W

Baranof
Island

866CS

Admiralty
Island

Kootznahoo
Inlet

900

Harbor Island

Kruzof
Island

Angoon

Hood
Bay

Stephens
Passage

Fords
Terror

Mount
Edgecumbe

Sitka

Five Finger
Light

Sitka
Sound

800W

Warm
Spring
Bay

840CS

Tyee

850

870

Frederick Sound

Kake

CHAPTER 7

Where History Lurks

JUNEAU, MILE 960, TO SITKA, MILE
815W, VIA SKAGWAY AND GLACIER BAY

*We came to a place where the water was covered with boards
and stuff. But there wasn't a soul left living to call to us for
help. Seemed like, just standing at the rail and looking at little
boards that had once been a ship and straining our eyes to
see folks that weren't there no more, and then looking at them
high mountains around Lynn Canal and thinking we had to
go over them and on beyond before we even got to the gold
country, quieted us all down. Somehow we didn't feel the
same way we'd been feeling on the trip up. That country up
there didn't look cordial. It made you feel like cutting out the
horseplay and saying a prayer for the fellows who wasn't there
no more, and for the rest of us who didn't know what was
ahead, neither.*

—*Martha Ferguson Mckeown,* The Trail Led North.

For the human throng bound for Skagway and the
Klondike in the Gold Rush years, the last 100 miles, from
Juneau to Skagway, were somber ones. The mountains
rise steeply from the water here and seem to funnel the wind.
Moreover, there is something about this landscape that humbles a person. Salmon fishermen bound north in their 30- to
40-foot gill-netters have a word for the vista north: "Looking
up at the Big Lynn."

Weather-bound mariners anchored in Auke Bay would

Joe Upton

Troller, Bridget Cove, mile 971N. The more austere landscape of Lynn Canal is evident here.

Look for sea lions at the rookery on Benjamin Island, east of mile 967N.

row ashore and hike out to Point Lena, **mile 956**, for their weather report — row after smoking row of gray-bearded seas, as another weather system funneled up or down the narrow canyon between these mountain walls.

The bottom is littered here with the pieces of two of the finest steamers to travel north. First was the *Princess Sophia*. At around 1 a.m. on October 24, 1918, the gold miners aboard and the crews of the 10 Yukon River paddle-wheelers were probably still celebrating. They'd left Skagway a few hours earlier, the rivers freezing up, their season over, the bright lights ahead.

Upstairs in the pilothouse, the atmosphere was more subdued, the captain anxious. He'd seen Eldred Rock Light, **mile 994**, at midnight through the snow but navigation on such a night relied on something called "time and compass." The skipper would calculate from the engine revolutions how fast his vessel was traveling. Taking his course line from the chart and making allowances for the wind and the tidal currents, he would steer until his time ran out, that is, when he should be at the next point of reference.

On that bitter night in 1918, with blowing snow and limited visibility, the next checkpoint after Eldred Rock was Sentinel Island Light, 28 miles away. Over such a distance, a steering error of one degree would put the vessel a half-mile off course.

Sometime around 2 a.m., as her skipper was groping through the snow and trying to see the Sentinel Island Light, the *Sophia* drove her whole length ashore on Vanderbilt Reef. Fortunately the rocks cradled her, and there was no need to try and launch lifeboats on such a rotten night.

By first light a rescue fleet was standing by: the *Cedar, King and Winge, Estebeth, Elsinore*, and others. But as the *Sophia* seemed to be resting securely on the rock, it was decided to wait until better weather to evacuate the passengers and crew.

It was a tragic mistake. In the late afternoon, the northerly began to blow with renewed fury, and the rescue fleet was forced to seek shelter in a nearby harbor. Darkness came, with driving snow and bitter wind, and the vessels had to set anchor watches to make sure they weren't dragging.

Lynn Canal is a notorious weather breeder in the fall.

Roaring down the canal, the wind caught the *Sophia*'s high exposed stern, opening up her plates and driving her off the reef and into the deep water beyond. There was time for one desperate radio call: "For God's sake come! We are sinking." In the morning only her masts were above water, her 343 passengers and crew drowned in the northwest coast's worst maritime disaster.

Thirty-four years later, miscalculation of a course change drove the graceful *Princess Kathleen* ashore at Lena Point, **mile 956**. Her passengers were more fortunate. They climbed down ladders to the rocky beach and watched the favorite of all Alaska-run steamers slide off the rocks and disappear into deep water.

Princess May, *on Sentinel Island, mile 966N, in 1910. She was lucky— there were no injuries, and she was refloated with little damage.*

Eldred Rock Light, mile 994N. Painting by Ann Upton, author's collection.

Look for Eldred Rock, the unusual octagonal lighthouse, reminiscent of Russian architecture, to the west at **mile 994N**. Here, on a morning in 1908 the light keepers were astonished to find part of the hull of the *Clara Nevada* that had been lost with 100 souls on a winter night a decade earlier. The seaweed-draped hull, still containing the bones of many victims, had been lifted from the canal floor and deposited on the rock by the storm the night before.

Look for glaciers in the valleys on both sides here. These small rivers of ice have receded from the salt water. Yet just 15 miles away over the mountain ridge to the west is Glacier Bay, full of floating ice.

"September 24, 1972, Twin Coves, Lynn Canal. Beach picnic tonight, with four other gill-netter families in here, our boats laying in the cove before us, the glaciers seeming to hang, glowing over us in the high latitude dusk. In the stillness after supper as we sat around the fire, there was a noise like thunder, and we looked up and saw house-size pieces of ice tumbling from Rainbow Glacier into the trees below."

Look carefully at the vegetation along the shores here. The spruce, cedar and hemlock are joined by deciduous trees

as the effect of latitude and the cold mainland land mass that surrounds the canal makes itself felt. Like in Juneau, the climate here is much more severe, much less moderated by the sea, than in Ketchikan or Sitka.

Northwest of Seduction Point at mile 1,002N (Vancouver named it after the natives had tried to lead his Lieutenant Whidbey into a trap.) is Chilkat Inlet, the last hurrah each season for salmon gill-netters. Into this narrow and steep-sided bay hundreds of thousands of chum salmon return each fall. As many as 450 vessels, each deploying a 900-foot-long net, will crowd into its barely six-square-mile area in a chaotic and competitive high-stakes frenzy. Along with the crowds, the fishermen have to fight the weather, for snow comes early to these northern fjords.

Substantial salmon runs return to the Chilkat River each fall.

"It came on hard, snow and wind, while we were still fishing. They hadn't yet pulled the floats for the winter in Cannery Cove, and the storm broke them all up. The smart guys quit fishing right with the first of the snow and headed for Haines, but we stayed until the fishing period was over. By that time it must have been blowing seventy out in the canal, and the fish buyers were huddled with us in two little coves. We were the last boat at the Emily Jane, our fish buyer, and the cannery was calling on the radio telling him to head on down to Petersburg, storm or not. They weren't

Fishermen's picnic, Chilkat Inlet, east of mile 1002N. Davidson Glacier on left, Rainbow Glacier at upper right.

Joe Upton

none too eager to go, and when they picked up the anchor and disappeared into the snow and the black, I wasn't sure I'd ever see him again."

—A Lynn Canal salmon fisherman.

Salmon that make it past the fishing fleet spawn each fall in the lower reaches of the Chilkat River, where thousands of bald eagles await their arrival. Look for eagles along the west side of the canal, especially in the fall. Possibly the largest concentration anywhere occurs around the shallow mouth of the Chilkat River, as the eagles feed on the carcasses of spawned-out chum salmon.

Haines and Port Chilkoot

The spot that looks like a New England village at mile 1,012N is Fort William H. Seward, sometimes known as Port Chilkoot. Decommissioned after World War II, it was purchased sight unseen by five veterans and their families to pursue their dream of a planned community. Now part of the city of Haines, just to the north, the fort offers a variety of cultural activities.

Haines, until a highway was recently completed out of Skagway, was the only place in southeastern Alaska with a road that went anywhere (it connected to the Alaska Highway). Today it is rich with Tlingit culture and is especially known for the dramatic fall migration of bald eagles that feed on Chilkat River salmon.

Part of old army fort at Port Chilkoot, mile 1012N.

JW Thwaites

Thwaites. 1256. *Mushers. Alaska.*

The Last Easy Miles

For the tens of thousands who came north during the
Gold Rush years, upper Lynn Canal represented the last easy
miles of their journey to the diggings.

As you enter Taiya Inlet at **mile 1,014N** from Seattle,
imagine yourself at the crowded rail of a ship like the *Queen*
or the *Victoria* in the fall of 1897, jostling for your place with
hundreds of other Klondikers, looking out through a snow
squall, trying to get a glimpse of what lay ahead. There was
but an hour or two before you must put on your pack, get
the boxes and sacks of your "outfit" (a year's worth of supplies) ready to unload, and step out into the wind and the
cold and whatever else fate had in store for you.

Much of the United States was gripped in a depression at
that time. Perhaps you were a farmer from the Dakotas; you
had left your family to try for fortune in the North. You had
bought your outfit in Seattle and steamer passage to Skagway, with little more knowledge than that somewhere
beyond those mountains men like yourself were staking out
gold claims and getting rich.

*Ready for the North.
Klondikers aboard
ship, 1897.*

The snow clears, and a cold and cheerless sun shines on as bleak and unfriendly a landscape as you've seen on this trip. The mountains seem to rise vertically out of the water; there doesn't even seem to be a beach. The chatter of the crowd fades as all look at the mountains and what lies ahead.

Note the steepness of the fjord walls.

If you were very lucky, your steamer tied to a wharf, but for those in the first wave in 1897, especially those at Dyea, six miles north of Skagway, which is now ruins on the beach, there were no wharves. Most gold seekers unloaded their outfits from steamers onto lighters, shallow-draft barges. If the tide was up, the lighters took you right in to shore. If it wasn't, the lighter got as far as the flats and you had to cross 200 or 300 yards of sand and mud to get to shore.

Many had brought animals and staked them out with their piles of boxes and gear while they made the first trips across the flats to shore.

Some weren't familiar with the big tides in the northern fjords of Alaska. They rested, perhaps, after lugging their first load up the beach, and visited with others about what they might expect in the rough hewn town, visible through the snow, and hiked back to find their outfit underwater, their animals drowned.

The steamers didn't wait; their owners wanted them back in Vancouver or Seattle as quickly as possible, "To get another load of suckers," as one bitter Klondiker put it.

The Gold Rush

For most of the hundred thousand or so who came north in 1897 and 1898, their Gold Rush experience had three phases. The first was often the hardest: the passes. The mountain wall that lay between the salt water of upper Lynn Canal and the edge of the Yukon had but two routes over it: Chilkoot Pass and White Pass.

The most powerful image from 1897 and 1898 is the long line of climbers, each bent with his load, on the steps cut into the ice on Chilkoot Pass. At the top lay the Canadian border and the North West Mounted Police. No one could pass without a year's supplies, about 1,500 pounds.

Wealthy men hired porters, but most just carried it all up themselves, load by backbreaking load, caching it at the top and hoping no one would rob them before they got back. On most days a solid stream of upward bound men filled the

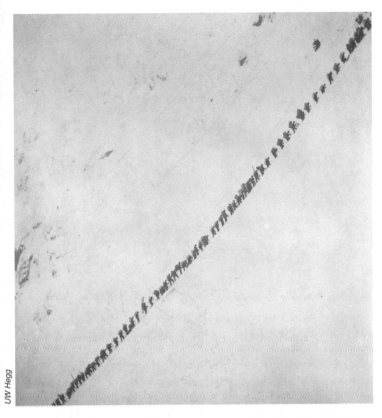

UW Hegg

Chilkoot Pass, 1897. If you stepped out of line to rest, it might be a long time before you could find a place to step in again.

steps. If you wanted to rest, you stepped off to the side, but when you wanted to get back in, you had to wait for a gap in the line; it was that crowded. By 1898 cable tramways could carry your gear over the pass for a fee, but the men in the first wave had only their feet.

Down the other side from the summit was Lake Bennett, and after that it was the boats and the rivers. They were 50 miles from salt water, but there was another 500 to the gold country. Arriving in winter, the men camped on the shore, cut down the trees, whipsawed them into planks and built boats, and waited for the ice to melt. As soon as the ice began to move, it was followed by all sorts of craft.

"Some leaked, some didn't steer. They had lots of things wrong with them. But a lot of the boats, made of whipsawed lumber, had beautiful lines and sailed as pretty as anything I ever did see on the Columbia. Yes, sir, that was an expedition, that fleet of boats getting ready to set out from Lake Bennett, come spring of '98." —Martha Ferguson Mckeown, *The Trail Led North.*

Down the canyons and through the rapids they came, the

UW HEGG 227

The first of the rapids: Once over the passes, the Klondikers cut trees, built boats, and faced 500 miles of rivers and rapids.

wealthier switching to Yukon steamers as soon as they could, but all heading for Dawson Creek and the last phase: the diggings.

The best claims were staked before most of the gold seekers arrived. Many who started north gave up before they got to the Yukon. Only half who made it staked a claim. Just a very few struck it rich. Most found some kind of work in Dawson City or in the diggings, made a little money, and moved on.

Yet their adventure transcends time. All experienced the powerful drama of the North. Those who returned, even penniless, brought back stories to entertain generations of breathless children and grandchildren.

To Sitka via Chatham and Peril Strait

Point Retreat, **mile 960**, was named by Vancouver's Lieutenant Whidbey after being repulsed by armed natives each time his party tried to land for the night, "where they drew up in battle array, with their spears couched, ready to receive our people on landing." —Captain George Vancouver, *A Voyage of Discovery*.

When I was a lad of 19, Point Augusta (**mile 904CS**) was where my first Alaskan skipper would turn over the wheel of the old salmon tender *Sidney* to me on our night runs from Icy Strait to Metlakatla.

The mate had bad eyes, the cook didn't steer, the insurance man's kid couldn't be trusted, and skipper liked his sleep. And so, after a long day of buying fish and attending to the mechanical problems of the Tsimshian seiners who fished for us, I'd sit up with the dark canyon of Chatham Strait opening ahead of me on the radar and a Seattle rock station fading in and out on the radio.

Sometimes there'd be the lights of another vessel, occasionally the wink of a navigational aid. But the land was always dark, and I remembered being stunned by it: all that land, all that waterfront, and hardly a town, a settlement, hardly even a house.

Tenakee Inlet, site of the settlement of Tenakee Springs, opens to the west at **mile 888CS**. The hot springs, 10 miles up the inlet, made it a popular wintering spot for many of the first prospectors and miners in the region.

Peril Strait, the inside route to Sitka, begins at mile **868CS**. The narrow part begins about an hour and a half later at Povorotni Island, **mile 896PS**. Pick a spot where you can see forward, because the ship will approach what seems like a dead end on the channel and then make a right-angle turn south between Chichagof and Baranof islands.

Look for Sergius Narrows at mile **903PS**. This is the narrowest part of Peril Strait; vessels wait for slack water to go through. How strong would the current be if it were moving?

The Lucky Few

With no convenient banks, many miners simply brought their gold south with them. One woman, hearing that her husband might be coming home on the steamer, brought their children to meet it, hoping he'd have enough money to buy them

Gold from Alaska at Scandinavian American Bank, Seattle, 1897.

MOHAI

groceries (he'd been gone six months and they were out of money). He staggered down the gangplank under the weight of his duffle and its 116 *pounds* of gold.

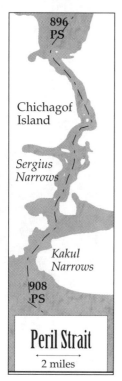

896'
PS

Chichagof
Island

Sergius
Narrows

Kakul
Narrows

908
PS

Peril Strait
← 2 miles →

Ferries and small
cruise ships go
through here. If
yours does, be on
deck!

Enough to suck the big navigational buoys completely under water.

Place names with the endings *-of, -oi, -ni, -shi*, such as Kruz*of* Island and Pogib*shi* Point, were given by the Russians, who claimed Alaska until 1867, when they sold it to the U.S.

You'll come into the open briefly at Salisbury Sound, after passing Kakul Narrows, mile **906PS**, but plunge again into riverlike Neva Strait at mile **913PS** and on into Olga Strait a few miles later. It's quite a trip. Imagine having to skipper a big ferry through here in fog or snow.

Look for Mount Edgecumbe, a flat-topped volcano visible to the southwest from around mile **923PS**. It's the traditional landfall for Asian lumber ships bound for the big mill at Sitka.

To Sitka via Icy Strait and Outside

When Vancouver's men explored here in July of 1794, they could barely get through Icy Strait because of the enormous amount of ice in the water. "The space between the shores on the northern and southern sides, seemed to be entirely occupied by one compact sheet of ice as far as the eye could distinguish." —Captain George Vancouver, *A Voyage of Discovery.*

Look for salmon seiners and trollers working these waters, as well as humpback whales. For many years Icy Strait has been the site of a very strong run of silver (coho) salmon. Trollers usually fish them with small, pastel-colored trolling spoons. A good day might be 200 fish, worth a thousand bucks or so to the fisherman.

The big inlet to the south at **mile 988** is Port Frederick. Around the point at the eastern entrance is a disused cannery and the Tlingit village of Hoonah. On the Fourth of July, salmon seiners put in here for one of the more boisterous celebrations in the region. Fishing used to be the community's bread and butter, but today logging on tribal lands is the primary revenue source. Much of the timber goes to Japan.

Hoonah is accessible by the smaller vessels of the Alaska ferry system, scheduled flights by two airlines, charter boats and planes (floatplanes and wheeled aircraft), and by cruise ships in the summer.

Stop at the L. Kane Store, founded in 1893, just 14 years after John Muir came to Glacier Bay. Hoonah's population is about 900, of which 80 percent are Tlingit. It is the largest

Tlingit settlement in Alaska, and the cultural center has a rich display of tribal art.

Look for whale-watching boats and humpback whales to the south near Point Adolphus.

You are 1,000 miles from Seattle. To the north at **mile 1,003** is Gustavus, a pleasant, un-southeastern spot: the land is flat and almost perfect for gardening. Farmers in the early part of the century grew vegetables here for the canneries at Excursion Inlet, Hawk Inlet, and other places. The Gustavus Inn offers lodging and family-style dining. Juneau residents take charter flights over for dinner. A road connects Gustavus with the Park Service headquarters for Glacier Bay at Bartlett Cove, 10 miles away.

Salmon troller Steve Snapp's Christmas card, 1995.

Glacier Bay

"Then setting sail, we were driven wildly up the fiord, as if the storm wind were saying, 'Go then, if you will, into my icy chamber; but you shall stay in until I am ready to let you out.' All this time sleety rain was falling on the bay and snow on the mountains; but soon after we landed the sky began to open. The camp was made on a rocky bench beneath the front of the Pacific Glacier, and the canoe was carried beyond the reach of the bergs and berg waves. The bergs were now crowded in a dense pack against the discharging front, as if the storm wind had determined to make the glacier take back her crystal offspring and keep them at home."

—John Muir, *Travels in Alaska.*

In the middle of October, 1879, John Muir and his missionary companion, a Mr. Young, set out from Fort Wrangell by canoe. With a crew of native paddlers, they were bound for the ice mountains of the north that prospectors had told

Continued on page 185

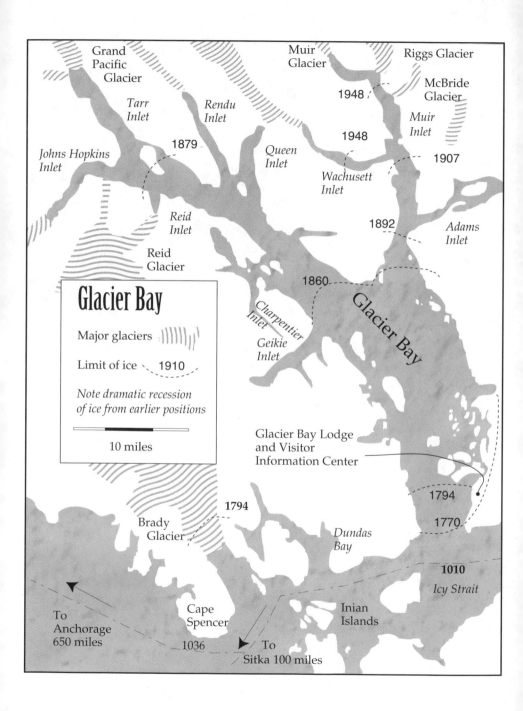

Grand
Pacific
Glacier

Muir
Glacier

Riggs Glacier

McBride
Glacier

*Tarr
Inlet*

*Rendu
Inlet*

1948

*Muir
Inlet*

*Johns Hopkins
Inlet*

1879

*Queen
Inlet*

1948

1907

*Wachusett
Inlet*

*Reid
Inlet*

1892

*Adams
Inlet*

Reid
Glacier

1860

*Charpentier
Inlet*

Glacier Bay

Glacier Bay

Major glaciers

Limit of ice ‐ 1910 ‐

*Note dramatic recession
of ice from earlier positions*

10 miles

*Geikie
Inlet*

Glacier Bay Lodge
and Visitor
Information Center

1794

1794

1770

Brady
Glacier

*Dundas
Bay*

1010

Icy Strait

To
Anchorage
650 miles

1036

Cape
Spencer

To
Sitka 100 miles

*Inian
Islands*

Christine Cox illustration

John Muir with Tlingit Paddlers, Glacier Bay, 1879

"We turned and sailed away, joining the outgoing bergs, while 'Gloria in excelsis' still seemed to be sounding over all the white landscape, and our burning hearts were ready for any fate, feeling that, whatever the future might have in store, the treasures we had gained this glorious morning would enrich our lives forever." (See story on page 186.)

—John Muir, *Travels in Alaska*

Skagway and Dyea, Winter, 1897

Klondikers, unloading gear onto the tide flats, hundreds of yards from shore at low tide.

The steamers didn't wait for high tide, when the men could have gotten their gear to dry land more easily. Their owners wanted them back in Vancouver or Seattle as quickly as possible, "To get another load of suckers," as one bitter Klondiker put it. (See story on page 170.)

Christine Cox illustration

Skagway, Winter 1897

For some, the challenge of the north—the cold, the difficult conditions, was simply too much:

"It was a real cold night. We walked along in the snow and we come to a fellow setting on the back of a Yukon sled. Yep, he was setting there in the middle of the road talking to hisself. His head was down on his hands. He looked plumb played out. He never seen us; he just went on talking to hisself. Over and over he'd say: 'It's hell. Yes; multiply it by ten and then multiply that by ten, and that ain't half as bad as this is. Yes, it's hell...'"

—Martha Mckeown, *The Trail Led North*

Christine Cox illustration

John Muir and Dog, on Brady Glacier, 1880

"...He looked up along the row of notched steps I had made, as if fixing them in his mind, then with a nervous spring he whizzed up and passed me out on the level ice and ran and cried and rolled about fairly hysterical in the sudden revulsion from the depth of despair to triumphant joy." (See story on page 189-190)

— John Muir, *Travels in Alaska*

Skagway

After Skagway and the passes, the wealthier men took steamboats down the Yukon.

It is the drama of '97 and '98 that fills this town. Skagway blossomed for but a few years, lawless and rough, then almost disappeared.

The gaunt-faced men have passed through to whatever fate the North had in store for them, but the town the boom built at the jumping-off place for the Klondike remains, much as it looked in 1897 and 1898, when some 80 saloons and many professional women were anxious to serve the lonely men on the trail north.

Today, Skagway offers a unique experience to visitors. Even the vegetation is different from the rest of Southeast Alaska, as the town is more under the influence of the harsher temperature extremes of the interior than the milder, cloudier maritime climate elsewhere in the region. Some of the native craftwork available here, especially of ivory, is unsurpassed in Alaska.

Helicopter Tours

Choppers are a great way to see the country, but they can be annoying to some residents, when the noisy machines drop down for a closeup of, say, a homestead. Try to put yourself in the position of someone who has come to Alaska seeking its beauty and peace to build a home. Having a helicopter hovering in your front yard several times a day is an aggravation. The pre-takeoff briefing might be a good time to suggest that you don't want to disturb anyone in your flight.

Skagway

2.

1.

THINGS TO DO:

1. **Downtown**—don't skip this— the atmosphere is authentic, the restaurants and shops excellent.

2. **See the pass**! The White Pass and Yukon Railroad, completed in 1899, represented victory in a tremendous struggle against bitter weather and forbidding mountains. Today the train follows the original route.

3.

4.

Russ Burtner Illustration

3. **Dyea,** at the trailhead for the dramatically steep Chilkoot Pass, didn't survive the post Gold Rush years. Hikers and bicyclists, however, are now discovering the trail.

4. **The Days of '98 Show** has been pleasing vistors for more than seventy years, and is a dramatic recreation of the events the town celebrates. Shows are generally timed to coincide with cruise ships visits.

Joe Upton

Steamer Prince
George *at
Skagway in 1973.*

SAM'S TOUR; "Ever since my dad showed me some old photos of the Gold Rush, I've always wanted to see Chilkoot Pass—not by chopper or plane, but to see it, even maybe hike the whole route. It's a tough hike for my old bones, and I didn't have the time this trip—the guide-books say allow for 3 to 5 days of strenuous going—but I just wanted to get a taste of it. So I rented a bike, checked in with the Park Service for trail conditions, had a great ride—six miles, along the water's edge. I parked my bike at the trailhead and just started, with a lunch pack, and an extra sweater. What a gorgeous trail—winding along the riverbank, but all I could think about was those who went before—you know, left their families behind, to make it in the North! I only went a couple hours in, ate and hiked out, but I made a vow: someday, I'll get in shape and do the whole thing! And that beer back at Moe's Frontier Bar, back in town, went down pretty smooth, too!"

ELSIE'S TOUR: "What a train ride—I did the whole thing, to Lake Bennett and back. I had thought that once the gold rush guys got over the pass, they were there! No way—turns out they still had another 500 miles to go—not only that, but most of them went over in winter and had to chop down trees, and handsaw planks to build boats to go down the rivers, after the ice melted—those guys were tough!

"I loved Skagway—I like the way they've got all those old buildings fixed up. I found this beautiful carved ivory cribbage board, with whaling ships and scenes all over it, almost like stuff you see in museums!"

Note: Only ivory harvested by native carvers in accordance with federal regulations may be legally sold. Make sure you get a export/transit permit if you buy ivory and plan to take it through customs when you return to the U.S.

Glacier Bay continued from page 175

Muir about. As they traveled, the youngest native, Sitka Charley, told Muir he'd hunted seals as a boy in a bay full of ice; he thought he could show Muir the way.

Even Muir was skeptical. Sitka Charley said the bay was without trees, that they'd need to bring their own firewood. The other paddlers, in all their lives throughout the region, had never seen a place without firewood.

They came to a bay cloaked in fog and storm. Sitka Charley became uneasy; the bay was much changed, he said, since he had seen it before. Even Vancouver's chart, a copy of which Muir so much relied upon, failed them, showing only a wide indentation in the shore.

Fortunately, they found a group of Hoonah seal hunters staying in a dark and crowded hut, who were getting in their winter's meat and skins. One of the men agreed to guide them, and northward they paddled, off the chart and into that astonishing bay that had been birthed from the ice almost within their lifetimes.

Look around and imagine yourself in a small canoe with native paddlers, as John Muir was in 1879.

The reason Vancouver had missed the bay was simple: it wasn't there. The front of the ice field extended almost to Icy Strait. Ninety years later when John Muir arrived, the front had retreated 45 miles, a half-mile a year.

The weather got worse, and Muir's paddlers wanted to turn around. "They seemed to be losing heart with every howl of the wind, and, fearing that they might fail me now that I was in the midst of so grand a congregation of glaciers, I made haste to reassure them that for ten years I had wandered alone among mountains and storms, and good luck always followed me, that with me, therefore, they need fear nothing. The storm would soon cease and the sun would shine to show us the way we should go, for God cares for us and guides us as long as we are trustful and brave, therefore all childish fear must be put away." —John Muir, *Travels in Alaska.*

And so on they went, camping at night in rain, on snowy beaches, pushing farther and farther, only glimpsing the vastness and grandeur of the land.

Finally Muir climbed the flanks of one of the mountains just as the clouds passed, and he gazed, stunned, at the grandeur and the size of the many-armed bay that was revealed below him.

When the party headed back, the lateness of the season

Photo by Laroche, collection of Dave Bohn, author of Glacier Bay, The Land and the Silence.

Steamer Queen at Muir Glacier, about 1890.

was evident. Each morning before they reached Icy Strait, the ice was frozen a little thicker, and the men had to cut a lane for their canoe with an axe and tent poles.

Muir's description of the moment of their departure is one of the icons of Alaskan literature:

"The green waters of the fiord were filled with sun spangles; the fleet of ice-bergs set forth on their voyages with the upspringing breeze; and on the innumerable mirrors and prisms of these bergs, and on those of the shattered crystal walls of the glaciers, common white light and rainbow light began to burn, while the mountains shone in their frosty jewelry, and loomed again in the thin azure in serene terrestrial majesty. We turned and sailed away, joining the outgoing bergs, while 'Gloria in excelsis' still seemed to be sounding over all the white landscape, and our burning hearts were ready for any fate, feeling that, whatever the future might have in store, the treasures we had gained this glorious morning would enrich our lives forever."

—John Muir, *Travels in Alaska.*

After Muir's discovery and powerful writings about what he'd seen, the bay became one of the premier sights of the Western hemisphere, becoming within a few years a regular stop for steamers such as the Ancon, the Idaho, and especially the *Queen*.

The destination for most was Muir Glacier, the face of which was an ice cliff towering above the decks of the approaching steamers, and calving up to 12 icebergs an hour.

Glacier Bay is a prime place for viewing humpback whales.

> "The Muir presented a perpendicular ice front at least 200 feet in height, from which huge bergs were detached at frequent intervals. The sight and sound of one of these huge masses of ice falling from the cliff, or suddenly appearing from the submarine ice-foot, was something which once witnessed was not to be forgotten. It was grand and impressive beyond description."
> —Fremont Morse, *National Geographic*, January, 1908.

At midday on September 10, 1899, as he was waiting for lunch at his salmon saltery in Bartlett Cove, August Buschmann was surprised to see his trunk come sliding across the floor at him. Moments later, the cook's helper came running into the building, frightened. He had been up on the hill at the native cemetery as the ground started to heave around him, and he thought the dead were coming to life.

The earthquake shattered the front of Muir Glacier and others, and within 48 hours Glacier Bay was a mass of floating ice so thick that ships could not reach the saltery at Bartlett Cove for two weeks. Icy Strait filled with ice, making Dundas Bay, 10 miles to the west, inaccessible.

It wasn't until the following July that the steamer Queen ventured close enough to Muir Inlet to see what had happened. The bay was still full of ice; only by picking their way

Glacier Bay Today

The ice has receded far since Muir's time, enlarging the inlet, and there is no glacier as dramatically accessible and active as Muir Glacier was. Still, the drama and stunning beauty of the place are compelling. Today, so many yachts and cruise ships visit Glacier Bay that the Park Service has begun to limit access to avoid disturbing the pack of humpback whales. Yet the place is truly magic: from even a large ship one may sense that the land, the ice and the water are much as they were when Muir saw the bay.

along the shore west of Willoughby Island could they make any progress. The closest they could get to Muir Glacier was 10 miles; the rest was solid ice. The next summer, steamers could approach to five miles.

Hidden behind a fleet of icebergs, Muir Glacier commenced a rapid retreat up the inlet; today the face is 25 miles north of where Muir found it.

What's wrong with this picture? Answer: Boat is in danger. Icebergs can topple suddenly as melting changes their center of gravity.

TIPS FOR MARINERS: Don't approach an iceberg or the face of a glacier too closely. A change in center of gravity caused by melting can cause large icebergs to capsize, and glaciers suddenly can drop chunks weighing thousands of tons into the water, causing great waves. And icebergs don't always fall; sometimes they come from the underwater foot of the glacier, surfacing suddenly and unexpectedly. Watch out for them!

Look southeast from **mile 1,024** into the cove between the Inian Islands, a favorite anchorage for purse seiners and tenders. Even in August, snow clings in the folds of the hills, almost to the water, and occasional icebergs drift among the anchored fleet at night.

"August 17, 1965, Inian Cove. Something woke me in the night, and I sat up in my bunk, wondering what it was. And then it came again, a faint but insistent scraping, as if another boat had drifted down on us in the night. I stumbled out on deck and, there, eerily lit by the three-quarter moon, was a big iceberg, moving gently down our port side, pushed by the tide. Its irregularly shaped top was even with my head; I reached out to touch it, to try and retrieve some of the gravel clearly visible within its pale, translucent flank. The gravel had been scraped off a canyon floor, hundreds of miles away, thousands of years before I was born. But the ice was hard, its contours softened by melting. My hand could find no purchase, and after a moment the berg moved away in the tide.

"Outside the point I saw a ghostly armada moving in the seven-knot current of North Inian Pass: eight or nine little bergs, maybe a thousand tons each, showing as big as medium-sized boats above the surface. In the moonlight they seemed to glow as if lit from within. I wanted to wake my shipmates, but then the tide pushed them around the corner and they were gone."

UW Thwaites 0036-4024

Look for tide rips northwest of the Inian Islands, near **mile 1,026**, as billions of gallons of water rush through constricted North Inian Pass.

The three-mile-wide indentation to the north at **mile 1,029** is Taylor Bay, leading to Brady Glacier at its head. Glaciologist extraordinaire Muir was here the summer after his 1879 Glacier Bay trip, hiking with a dog over the flats and up to Brady Glacier on a cold and rainy August day. In the late afternoon, he had to take a running jump across a very wide crevasse. Fortunately the other side was lower, but even so he barely made it; a few minutes later he realized he and the dog had jumped onto a sort of island, surrounded by wide and deep crevasses. The only ways out were back across the crevasse that he had barely made jumping down, or across a frighteningly precarious ice bridge, curved, drooping, knife-edged, eight feet down in the abyss of a crevasse from the surface of the glacier.

Muir chose the ice bridge, notching steps into the side of the crevasse, and sliding across, straddling the top, chipping away the sharp-edged top as he went so that the dog could also use it. As he worked, the dog whimpered and cried, refusing to follow.

Only with difficulty did he set across. It began to get dark, and Muir could wait no longer. He made to go away, calling out to the dog that he could make it if he only tried.

"Finally, in despair, he hushed his cries, slid his little feet slowly down into my footsteps out on the big sliver,

Steamer Northwestern, 1898. In extreme cases, iced up vessels capsized from the increased weight.

UW THWAITES 0308-1

Port Althorp Cannery (south of mile 1029), around 1930. Today, only a few pilings on the beach mark its site.

walked slowly and cautiously along the sliver as if holding his breath, while the snow was flying and the wind was moaning and threatening to blow him off. When he arrived at the foot of the slope below me, I was kneeling on the brink ready to assist him in case he should be unable to reach the top. He looked up along the row of notched steps I had made, as if fixing them in his mind, then with a nervous spring he whizzed up and passed me out on to the level ice and ran and cried and rolled about fairly hysterical in the sudden revulsion from the depths of despair to triumphant joy. I tried to catch him and pet him and tell him how good and brave he was, but he would not be caught. He ran round and round, swirling like autumn leaves in an eddy, lay down and rolled head over heels."

—John Muir, *Travels in Alaska.*

Look for fishing boats coming out of the community of Elfin Cove, southeast of mile 1,029. This tiny settlement, with its boardwalk and its anchored fish buyers, is the center for the salmon trollers working this area.

The conspicuous lighthouse to the north at **mile 1,036**, less than a half hour past Taylor Bay, is Cape Spencer Light, which marks the end of the Inside Passage. From here on northward, travel is along an unfriendly and exposed coast. From Cape Spencer to Prince William Sound, 400 miles northwest, there is only a single harbor, Yakutat Bay, where a vessel may take refuge.

In winter, the trip across the Gulf of Alaska (straight-line to Kodiak Island) or along the coast can be difficult indeed. One of the most feared hazards is icing, the heavy accumulation of salt water ice that occurs when a vessel is traveling rough seas in cold weather. The bugaboo is weight: in heavy icing the vessel's center of gravity rises until the vessel is at risk of capsizing. The best solution is usually to turn away from the wind to reduce flying spray and send the crew out with baseball bats and hammers to knock the ice off.

"We were coming up on Spencer northbound, and the skipper called down to the galley for us to come up and have a look at something. At first I thought it was an iceberg; only when it got closer did we recognize it as a boat. It was spooky, just looking at it. All the antennas were busted off, and there was plywood over three of the pilothouse windows. The crew were all out on deck, knocking off ice and shoveling it over the side. They must have had a hell of a crossing."

—An Alaskan crab fisherman.

Outside Waters: Cape Spencer to Sitka

Much of the next 80 miles down the outside coast to Sitka takes us past wild, remote country, guarded by reefs, little visited except by fishermen. The rock piles in this area, as reefs are frequently called, pose a particular challenge to trollers, as many king salmon feed along this coast in the summer.

By using their sounding machines in conjunction with "ranges" on shore—lining up two points, say a particularly tall tree with a mountaintop, to give a line of position—experienced trollers are able to "fly" their gear through the complex series of underwater mountain ranges and valleys. Often the fisherman who is able to maneuver his gear closest to the bottom gets the most fish. If he gets too close, however, he is liable to "hang up," causing an expensive loss of gear.

These rugged shores are popular with trollers.

It was along this rocky shore that the crew of the *Maggie Murphy* finally began to make some desperately needed money. "For seven wonderful days, our only worry was the problem of finding a safe storage for the handfuls of money paid us by the buyers...."

"Work! We scarcely stopped to eat or sleep... Each day, we fished until midnight, sold to the buyer, snatched a brief nap, then returned to toil on the ocean. For a full seven days, we did not cook, wash, or change clothes. Fish blood and slime colored our clothing and specked our faces. The cabin became littered with discarded equipment and tracked with fish offal. The pitching of the boat inflicted scores of bruises on us, and our senses were dulled from lack of sleep. But the filthiness of our boat was a trifle, and our weary bodies be damned. We just caught fish, sold them, and caught more.

"The prime object of each buyer was to outdo the others in extending favors to the fishermen and thereby capture the majority of the boats in the harbor as customers. When we drew up to a buying boat at night, attendants would seize the *Maggie Murphy* and lash it alongside in the crisp, courteous manner of a service station operator. Then they would board our boat and pitch the fish onto the scales for us. The fish would be graded and weighed, and we would be paid in cash to the nearest dollar, with the difference in our favor. If we wanted groceries, we had only to shout our order and the food would be laid on deck. We were charged for the groceries to the nearest dollar, with any difference again in our favor. There was no change circulating in the booming business channels of this harbor. Invariably, as we shoved off, the buyer would give us some sort of a bonus, such as a handful of candy bars, or a paper sack full of beer stubbies."

—John Joseph Ryan, *The Maggie Murphy*.

Look for heavily eroded shores — evidence of violent winter storms.

Look for Lisianski Strait, visible to the northeast from about **mile 867W**, one of many sheltered shortcuts available to small craft traveling from Icy Strait to Sitka. Such vessels travel outside for 30 miles, then enter Salisbury Sound, **mile 840W**, and continue through the narrow Neva and Olga straits to Sitka.

Southbound cruise ships, however, generally stay outside, turning to enter Sitka Sound at Cape Edgecumbe, **mile 815W**.

Look for Mount Edgecumbe, the 3,271-foot flat-topped volcanic cone that marks the entrance to Sitka Sound. Notice the black volcanic rocks and cliffs in this vicinity, a significant landmark for mariners.

Joe Upton

TIPS FOR MARINERS: Approaching Sitka in thick weather? Look for the color of the cliffs if you get a glimpse of the shore. If it's black, then you're north of the entrance to Sitka Sound. If it's whitish gray, then you're south.

Sitka to Vancouver via Outside Waters

The vessel follows in reverse the outside route to Sitka to Cape Ommaney, then goes offshore, offering a good view of dramatic Helm Point. This is the most conspicuous headland in southeastern Alaska, an almost vertical 1,000- foot cliff at **mile 727W**. (See more on page 135.)

TIPS FOR MARINERS: Approaching Coronation Island in thick weather without radar? Use your horn or whistle: the cliffs on either side of Windy Bay give good echoes.

The high land to the east here is all Prince of Wales Island. Small craft use narrow, dredged, El Capitan Passage to get to the rich salmon grounds in Sea Otter Sound, northeast of **mile 720W**, and Noyes Island, **mile 705W**.

The area between Cape Addington, **mile 700W**, and Cape Bartolome, **mile 685W** is a favorite spot for trollers seeking king salmon. Before the seasons were limited in the late 1970s, outside trolling opened on April 15, and many small vessels would beat their way up the coast from Puget Sound to be there for it.

It was, as they say, a tough berth. Trollers anchored for the night at Steamboat Bay on Noyes Island and then headed out through the tide rips at Cape Ulitka to the outside. Consider these excerpts from my 1974 log:

Cape Addington: "That's an evil place, and we gave it plenty of room in order to stay clear of the tide race, but even so, it was a wild hour before we were around."

Joe Upton

"April 29. Steamboat Bay cannery. Day came at 3 a.m. with violent squalls heeling us over at the float. Pulled on oilskins and ran a long bow line out to the float, then back in the sack for some good winks with the eerie whine of the wind loud around us.

"April 30. Headed out to Cape Ulitka, where the ocean pours around the point and meets the outgoing tide. That's a dirty spot; we almost turned around right there. The swells on the outside were 15 feet high, mean and ominous in the early morning light with a wind chop on top.

"If you only see Cape Addington once, it should be on such a day. The wind was coming on hard and running against the tide, and the cape, a long rocky arm, was almost lost in the mists as the heavy seas beat against its rocky sides, That's an evil place, and we gave it plenty of room in order to stay clear of the tide race, but even so, it was a wild hour before we were around. Once, on top of a big one, I took a long look around. To the south, the water was white and the sky was dark. A quarter-mile away, Doug labored through the rip, but beyond that we were alone. There was nothing but the sky and the troubled sea.

"May 9. At anchor, Paloma Pass. Today the seas drove white around the point and beat on the rocks off our stern, but in the lee we were secure, our world bounded by the dark shores and the racing clouds above. Neither on this island nor

Workers' cabins, Waterfall Cannery, 1973. In its new life as a fishing lodge, Waterfall Resort, northeast of mile 680W, is one of the showpieces of southeastern Alaska.

most of the islands around is there any sign of man. Saw one boat yesterday, none today; tried to get music on the radio but there was only the hiss of static."

Behind Suemez Island, northeast of mile **680W**, is Waterfall Resort, better known to generations of salmon fishermen and travelers as Waterfall Cannery. It was the showpiece of the southeastern Alaska salmon industry in the 1940s and 1950s. Supporting a fleet of boats and several hundred cannery workers as well as a full-time gardener, it canned fish caught in fish traps, including a trap at Cape Addington.

Though difficult to recognize as a separate island, the land to the east, from **mile 680W** all the way to Cape Muzon, **mile 635W**, is Dall Island, uninhabited, behind which is a complex of waterways and islands, including Cordova Bay, that are popular fishing spots for salmon purse seiners in July and August. This is wild, rugged, isolated country. Some of these bays might not see a human being from October through May.

Look for salmon purse seiners fishing for pink and sockeye salmon off these shores. After dark, look for the twinkle of anchor lights in these bays and coves.

From Cape Muzon, Vancouver-bound vessels usually join the Hecate Strait route south at **mile 575W** or the regular Inside Passage track around **mile 595**.

First snow, author's cabin at Point Baker, 1973.

Author's Note

Ships and ferries are a great way to see the Inside Passage and northwest coast. Amidst the enjoyment of traveling in such craft, it is easy to forget that for many thousands of fishermen, mariners, and their families, the Inside Passage is the highway between their homes and their workplaces. In spring and fall especially, when the weather has turned against the traveler, the highway can be rough indeed. In 1974, for instance, we caught our last fish near mile 1,000 on October 9 in a mean 40-knot breeze, and it took us three days of difficult traveling to get back to our cabin at Point Baker. I remember my feelings the night we arrived.

"Point Baker, 10 p.m., October 12, 1974. Ran three days to get here, most through ugly weather. Hardly saw another boat, or house; spent both nights in lonely and wild spots. Today ran through Rocky Pass (north of mile 745) with the last of the light and a few ducks and geese trading back and forth, and finally across Sumner Strait, to tie once again to our little float in a black and empty cove.

"Everything was as we had left it (we'd been away six weeks) except the skiff had sunk. We bailed it out and rowed ashore. Our dog went off to sniff around his old haunts, and we lit the kerosene lamps, built a fire in the wood stove, and found the rum.

"Outside the wind began again, working at a loose shingle like a dog at a bone, and our lights shone out on the wild and unfriendly night. We'd made our winter money, and our lives seemed filled up in a way they never did in the south."

Sitka

When Juneau was woods and snow and Ketchikan was a summer village of the Tlingit people, Sitka residents enjoyed theater, fine wines, and all the riches that the sea otter trade provided her Russian residents.

It was a trade based on the sometimes unwilling participation of the native people. In the Aleutian Islands, for example, the *promyshlenniki*, as the Russian fur traders were called, had no qualms about destroying whole villages if the Aleut residents didn't quickly obey them.

At Sitka, the proud Tlingit people cared little for the Russians, and in 1802 they destroyed the first Russian outpost, north of the present town site. Two years later the Russians returned with three ships and many Aleut mercenaries in kayaklike bidarka boats. Finally routing the Tlingits, the Russians reestablished Sitka on the site of the Tlingit village, Shee Atika.

For much of its Russian history, Sitka's leader was Aleksandr Baranov, who established schools for the Tlingits and made Sitka the trading capital of the northwest coast.

Fortunately for the Americans, the Russians' enlightenment didn't extend to conserving the valuable fur resource, for once the sea otter had been slaughtered almost to extinction, financial reverses made the Russians willing to sell Alaska to the United States for $7.2 million, about 2 cents an acre, which they did in 1867.

Left: totem at Sitka National Historical Park, located along the waterfront about a half mile south of town. *Above:* the Pioneer Home dominates the downtown waterfront, which is convenient as many of its residents are ex-fishermen. *Below*: many smaller vessels approach Sitka through the narrow waters of Peril Strait. If your vessel transits this passage early, make sure you get up for its dramatic scenery.

Sitka Scrapbook

Above left: the dome of St. Michael's Cathedral celebrates the strong influence of the early Russian occupation of this part of Alaska. *Above:* if you want to catch a salmon, Sitka's nearby ocean waters are an excellent place to try. *Left:* a young Sitka fiddler welcomes visitors

Today, having missed the booms and busts of the gold rush, Sitka, way out on the ocean side of Baranof Island, is the cultural center of southeastern Alaska. Yet Sitka offers more than museums and vistas; there are many things to do:

Sitka is home port to a large fleet of salmon trollers and halibut and codfish longliners.

•GO FISHING: If you have any inclination to try for a salmon or halibut, Sitka is an excellent place to go out on one of the charter vessels. The city's unique position on the outside coast and the strong runs of king and silver salmon make the chances of getting a fish here very high. Such a trip is also an opportunity to see close-up the dramatic coast of Alaska and its sea life and wildlife.

•JET BOATS: Advances in vessel design and propulsion have made an unusual experience available at Sitka: the high-speed jet boats. Propelled by water jets (essentially large pumps) rather than conventional propellers, these impressive craft allow passengers to travel quickly to places such as Salisbury Sound, 25 miles north of town. The abundant wildlife populations make it likely you'll see a whale, bear, or sea otter (today protected by federal law).

•THE SHELDON JACKSON MUSEUM: In his travels through the state as education agent, Dr. Jackson acquired a remarkable collection of native art and historical artifacts. Even if you have seen other such displays, you will find this collection unusually complete and worth seeing. The Aleut and Eskimo exhibits are particularly fascinating, with material such as their rain gear made of walrus intestines.

•ALASKA RAPTOR REHABILITATION CENTER: A place where injured hawks, falcons, owls, and eagles (mostly eagles) are cared for, this volunteer-run facility lets visitors view the dramatic birds close-up.

•SITKA NATIONAL HISTORICAL PARK: If you didn't get to Totem Bight or Saxman at Ketchikan and want to get a good view of totem poles, this is a close-to-downtown opportunity to do so. Set among trees in a dramatic walk along the shore, the 15 totems are "recarves" of poles col-

lected from Prince of Wales Island at the turn of the century. Cedar totems have a life of about 100 years out exposed to the elements.

• THE RUSSIAN BISHOP'S HOUSE AND ST. MICHAEL'S CATHEDRAL: Both downtown, these are culturally rich, dramatic elements of Sitka's Russian period. The Bishop's House is the original 1842 structure; the cathedral is a replica of the one destroyed by fire in 1966 (much of the artwork was saved).

ELSIE'S TOUR: "Do the Sheldon Jackson Museum! I had absolutely no idea of the intricacy of the native cultures. The sleds, the skin boats, the kayaks—it just makes one very humble to realize how well they were able to get around before we created our gasoline-powered world. They made everything—one of the neatest things on display was an Eskimo woman's tool case made out of fish skin."

Steamer City of Topeka at Sitka wharf, circa 1905. Note sealing schooner anchored in islands, and Mount Edgecumbe, faintly visible at right top.

Traveler's Guide to Marine Mammals

BELUGA WHALE. Size: to 18 feet. Range: Arctic waters. Occasionally to Bristol Bay, Alaska. Distinguishing features: Adults are pure white; juveniles are gray. Likes coastal waters, especially rivers. Especially likes codfish, but also crabs and mussels. Frequently seen in groups. History: Nicknamed "sea canary" because of extensive vocalizing.

BOWHEAD WHALE. Size: 45 to 60 feet, weight to 100 tons or more. Range: Arctic waters. Distinguishing features: Very large head, black with white chin. Plankton eater, skims schools with top of head just above surface. History: A staple of Eskimo diet. Once hunted extensively for its baleen, used in corsets.

HUMPBACK WHALE. Size: 30 to 50 feet, weight to 40 tons. Range: Throughout Alaska and British Columbia in summer. Winters in warm waters. Distinguishing features: Black with white throat and belly, long tail flipper with irregular edges. Knobs and bumps on head and flippers. Likes to breach, or jump dramatically. History: Much studied, commonly seen, sings hauntingly.

GRAY WHALE. Size: 30 to 50 feet. Range: coastal Arctic to Mexico. Distinguishing features: Black with white spots and blotches. Only large whale with overhanging upper jaw. Sometimes pokes head vertically out of water; also breaches. History: Calves its young in one of several lagoons in Baja California after annual migration. Whale watchers count them on their journey.

ORCA, OR KILLER WHALE. Size: to 30 feet. Range: global, especially coastal. Distinguishing features: Bold black and white markings, dramatic tall dorsal fin, especially on male. History: Before 1970s thought to be dangerous to man. Captured whales showed remarkable intelligence and docility. Many in aquariums. Travel and live in pods, or groups.

STELLER'S, OR NORTHERN SEA LION. Size: to 13 feet and 2,400 pounds. Range: California to Alaska; often found in large numbers at remote rookeries. Distinguishing features: Large size, visible ears, bad breath, and occasional loud roaring. History: Now protected by law, these large mammals are commonly seen along the Alaska coast. Eats fish, particularly salmon, to the annoyance of man.

HARBOR SEAL. Size: 4 to 6 feet. Range: Throughout most of the northwest coast. Distinguishing features: Grayish with spots; the most common seal in Alaska. Has no visible ears; clumsy on land. History: Fish and shellfish eaters, they frequently steal salmon from fishermen's nets and lines. Protected by law.

DALL PORPOISE: Size: 4 to 7 feet. Range: Throughout most northwest waters. Distinguishing features: Black body with dramatic white markings, small triangular dorsal fin. Sometimes mistaken for killer whales, but are much smaller with lower dorsal fin. Usually travels in groups. History: Likes to ride the bow waves of fishing and other craft.

Alert Bay, British Columbia, 1910.

A Northern Journal

Vancouver Island, British Columbia, 1905

A Northern Journal

Desolation Sound, British Columbia

A Northern Journal

Cook Inlet, Alaska

A Northern Journal

Point Baker, Alaska

A Northern Journal

Point Baker, Alaska

A Northern Journal

Killisnoo Island, Alaska, 1974

A Northern Journal

Acknowledgments

I am indebted to a number of unusually talented people, without whom this book would have been far less than what it is.

In particular to my designer, Martha Brouwer, of Waterfront Press, for her skill and grace in taking a sheaf of text, maps and drawings and fashioning them page by page into art.

To illustrator and artist extraordinaire Christine Cox for her gorgeous drawings, and her patience in working with me.

To illustrator and computer artist Russ Burtner, for taking my crude drawings and making them into exciting art.

To Barbara Bennett for allowing me to share the unusual talent of her father, Elton Bennett, with this book's readers.

To artists John Horton, Rie Munoz, Marvin Oliver, Nancy Stonington and Ray Troll for their very special talents and for alowing me to use examples of their fine work.

To my old pen pals, John and Peggy Hanson, for their ideas, and valuable suggestions.

To John J. O'Ryan, for allowing me to quote freely from his great book, *The Maggie Murphy*.

To Doug Charles of the Tongass Historical Society for so generously sharing the society's fine collection of early Alaska photographs.

To my editor Ed Reading, for his careful and patient guidance.

To John Pappenheimer, of Waterfront Press, for his continual support, excitement and direction.

To my family, for encouraging me through a long project.

To many friends and shipmates, in all manner of craft, in many a breezy cove and strait, for sharing so many stories of the coast.

And finally to old Mickey Hansen, passed away but not forgotten, for his kindness in taking a greenhorn kid under his wing aboard the old *Sydney*, in 1965, showing him the way of a ship and the magic of the North.

Bibliography

Armstrong, Robert H. *A Guide to the Birds of Alaska*. Bothel: Alaska Northwest Books, 1991.

Blanchet, M. Wylie. *The Curve of Time*, North Vancouver: Whitecap Books Ltd., 1990.

Bohn, Dave. *Glacier Bay: The Land and the Silence*. New York: Ballantine Books, 1967.

Bolotin, Norm. *Klondike Lost*. Anchorage: Alaska Northwest Publishing, 1980.

Bonnett, Wayne. *A Pacific Legacy*. San Francisco: Chronicle Books, 1991.

Browning, Robert. *Fisheries of the North Pacific*. Anchorage: Alaska Northwest Publishing, 1974.

Canadian Hydrographic Service: *British Columbia Pilot, Vol I & II* . Ottawa, 1965, 1969.

Craven, Margaret. *I Heard the Owl Call My Name*. New York: Doubleday Books, 1972

DuFresne, Jim. *Glacier Bay National Park*. Seattle: The Mountaineers Books, 1987.

Egan, Timothy. *The Good Rain*. New York: Alfred A. Knopf, 1990.

Eppenbach, Sarah. *Alaska's Southeast*. Seattle: Pacific Search Press, 1990.

Farwell, Captain R.F. *Captain Farwell's Hansen Handbook*. Seattle: L&H Printing, 1951.

Gibbs, Jim. *Disaster Log of Ships*. Seattle: Superior Publishing, 1971.

Graham, Donald. *Lights of the Inside Passage*. Madeira Park: Harbour Publishing, 1986.

Hill, Beth. *Upcoast Summers*. Ganges: Horsdal & Schubart, 1985.

Hoyt, Erich. *Orca: the Whale Named Killer*. Buffalo: Firefly Press, 1990.

Iglauer, Edith. *Fishing With John*. New York: Farrar, Straus & Giroux, 1988.

Jackson, W.H. *Handloggers*. Anchorage: Alaska Northwest Publishing, 1974.

Jacobsen, Johan Adrian. *Alaskan Voyage 1881-1883*. Chicago: University of Chicago Press, 1977.

Jonaitis, Aldona, editor. *Chiefly Feasts*. Seattle: University of Washington Press, 1991.

Jonaitis, Aldona. *From the Land of the Totem Poles*. Seattle: University of Washington Press, 1988.

Larssen, A.K., and Sig Jaeger. *The ABC's of Fo'c's'le Living.* Seattle: Madrona Publishers, 1976.

Macfie, Matthew. *Vancouver Island and British Columbia.* London: 1865.

McIntyre, Joan. *Mind in the Waters.* New York: Charles Scribner's Sons, 1974.

Mckeown, Martha. *The Trail Led North: Mont Hawthorne's Story.* Portland, Oregon: Binfords & Mort, 1960.

Muir, John. *Travels in Alaska.* Boston: Houghton, Mifflin Co., 1915.

Newell, Gordon and Joe Williamson. *Pacific Tugboats.* Seattle: Superior Publishing, 1957.

Nicholson, George. *Vancouver Island's West Coast.* Victoria: Moriss Printing, 1965.

Price, Andrew, Jr. *Port Blakely.* Seattle: Port Blakely Books, 1989.

Ritter, Harry. *Alaska's History.* Bothel: Alaska Northwest Books, 1993.

Rushton, Gerald. *Echoes of the Whistle.* Vancouver: Douglas & McIntyre, 1980.

Ryan, John J. *The Maggie Murphy.* New York: W.W. Norton & Co., 1951.

U.S. Dept. of Commerce. *United States Coastal Pilot, Vol 8 & 9.* Washington, D.C. 1969.

Upton, Joe. *Alaska Blues.* Anchorage: Alaska Northwest Publishing, 1977.

Upton, Joe. *Journeys Through the Inside Passage.* Bothel: Alaska Northwest Books, 1992.

Vancouver, George. *A Voyage of Discovery to the North Pacific Ocean and Round the World.* London: 1798.

Walbran, Captain John T. *British Columbia Coast Names.* Ottawa: Government Printing Bureau, 1909.

Weinstein, Robert A. *Tall Ships on Puget Sound.* Seattle: University of Washington Press, 1978.

White, Howard, and Jim Spilsbury. *The Accidental Airline.* Madeira Park: Harbour Publishing, 1988.

White, Howard, editor. *Raincoast Chronicles: Forgotten Villages of the B.C. Coast.* Madeira Park: Harbour Publishing, 1987.

Index

Traveling northwest waters since 1965 in
small craft and large, Joe Upton gained intimate knowledge of the coast from Puget
Sound almost to the Arctic Circle.

In the 1970s Upton lived and fished out
of a small wilderness island community in
Southeast Alaska. His first book, *Alaska
Blues*, based on those years, was hailed as
"One of those books you want to proclaim a
classic" by the *Seattle Post Intelligencer*.

Presently Upton lives with his wife and
two children on an island in Puget Sound,
and spends much of his summers traveling
and fishing along the northwest coast.